"In this movement throu
nurture my wife, and I w
also let me gaze at even bi~~~~~ ~~~~~~~
how it is by Jesus, for him, and to him."

Ed Welch, counselor and faculty, Christian Counseling and Educational Foundation

"Captivating, alluring, and tearfully rendered, Ray Ortlund's *Marriage and the Mystery of the Gospel* displays the blood-bought gift of biblical marriage amidst the splendor of the whole biblical landscape. No polemics here—just the love of God poured out to conquer hell itself. Each page shows the biblical worldview in its aesthetic loveliness and disarming power. And don't let the title fool you. This is not just another book on marriage. Readers will drink in a tour de force of biblical majesty on display on each and every page."

Rosaria Butterfield, author, *The Secret Thoughts of an Unlikely Convert*

"Ray Ortlund brilliantly enables you to carefully examine your marriage through the lenses of creation, fall, law, and gospel. In so doing, he helps us deepen our understanding of marriage, know why it is a struggle for us all, diagnose the marriage confusion in our culture, be clear where marriage help is to be found, and fall in love all over again with our God of amazing love, wisdom, and grace."

Paul David Tripp, President, Paul Tripp Ministries; author, *What Did You Expect?*

"*Marriage and the Mystery of the Gospel* lifts our eyes above the contemporary debates over complementarianism and egalitarianism, feminism and patriarchy, same-sex unions, and divorce and remarriage. Ortlund places our focus on the glory of the cosmic love story and the joy-filled hope this story offers for finding true romantic love in a fallen world. This is biblical theology at its best."

Eric C. Redmond, Assistant Professor of Bible, Moody Bible Institute

"There is no one alive I would rather read than Ray Ortlund. This book will show you why. It shows us how marriage is a metaphor for the gospel itself, the one-flesh union of Christ to his church. This book will help you see both the gospel and marriage in a clearer light, in the light of an unveiled mystery."

Russell Moore, President, Ethics & Religious Liberty Commission of the Southern Baptist Convention

"Robert Wolgemuth and I asked Ray Ortlund to preach on marriage as a picture of redemption at our wedding. We know him to be a pastor with a scholar's head and a lover's heart. And we admire his marriage as a beautiful picture of the passionate, tender love relationship between Christ and his church. For the same reasons, I commend to you this book. It will deepen your understanding of the divine mystery of marriage and why it matters, and it will inflame your heart to pursue greater love and oneness with Christ and with your mate."

Nancy DeMoss Wolgemuth, author; Radio Host, *Revive Our Hearts*

Marriage

and the Mystery of the Gospel

Ray Ortlund

Dane C. Ortlund and Miles Van Pelt,
series editors

:: CROSSWAY®

WHEATON, ILLINOIS

Marriage and the Mystery of the Gospel

Copyright © 2016 by Raymond C. Ortlund Jr.

Published by Crossway
  1300 Crescent Street
  Wheaton, Illinois 60187

Cover design: Pedro Oyarbide

First printing 2016

Printed in the United States of America

Trade paperback ISBN: 978-1-4335-4687-7
ePub ISBN: 978-1-4335-4690-7
PDF ISBN: 978-1-4335-4688-4
Mobipocket ISBN: 978-1-4335-4689-1

Library of Congress Cataloging-in-Publication Data

Names: Ortlund, Raymond C., Jr., author.
Title: Marriage and the mystery of the Gospel / Ray Ortlund.
Description: Wheaton, Illinois : Crossway, 2016. | Series: Short studies in biblical theology series | Includes bibliographical references and index.
Identifiers: LCCN 2016019913 (print) | LCCN 2016023839 (ebook) | ISBN 9781433546877 (tp) | ISBN 9781433546884 (pdf) | ISBN 9781433546891 (mobi) | ISBN 9781433546907 (epub)
Subjects: LCSH: Marriage—Biblical teaching. | Marriage—Religious aspects—Christianity.
Classification: LCC BS680.M35 O78 2016 (print) | LCC BS680.M35 (ebook) | DDC 261.8/3581—dc23
LC record available at https://lccn.loc.gov/2016019913

Crossway is a publishing ministry of Good News Publishers.

BP		29	28	27	26	25	24	23	22	21	20	19
15	14	13	12	11	10	9	8	7	6	5	4	3

For my wife

Short Studies in Biblical Theology

Edited by Dane C. Ortlund and Miles V. Van Pelt

The City of God and the Goal of Creation, T. Desmond Alexander (2018)

Covenant and God's Purpose for the World, Thomas R. Schreiner (2017)

From Chaos to Cosmos: Creation to New Creation, Sidney Greidanus (2018)

The Kingdom of God and the Glory of the Cross, Patrick Schreiner (2018)

The Lord's Supper as the Sign and Meal of the New Covenant, Guy Prentiss Waters (2019)

Marriage and the Mystery of the Gospel, Ray Ortlund (2016)

The Son of God and the New Creation, Graeme Goldsworthy (2015)

Work and Our Labor in the Lord, James M. Hamilton Jr. (2017)

Contents

Series Preface

Most of us tend to approach the Bible early on in our Christian lives as a vast, cavernous, and largely impenetrable book. We read the text piecemeal, finding golden nuggets of inspiration here and there, but remain unable to plug any given text meaningfully into the overarching storyline. Yet one of the great advances in evangelical biblical scholarship over the past few generations has been the recovery of biblical theology—that is, a renewed appreciation for the Bible as a theologically unified, historically rooted, progressively unfolding, and ultimately Christ-centered narrative of God's covenantal work in our world to redeem sinful humanity.

This renaissance of biblical theology is a blessing, yet little of it has been made available to the general Christian population. The purpose of Short Studies in Biblical Theology is to connect the resurgence of biblical theology at the academic level with everyday believers. Each volume is written by a capable scholar or churchman who is consciously writing in a way that requires no prerequisite theological training of the reader. Instead, any thoughtful Christian disciple can track with and benefit from these books.

Each volume in this series takes a whole-Bible theme and traces it through Scripture. In this way readers not only learn about a given theme but also are given a model for how to read the Bible as a coherent whole.

We are launching this series because we love the Bible, we love the church, and we long for the renewal of biblical theology in the academy to enliven the hearts and minds of Christ's disciples all around the world. As editors, we have found few discoveries more thrilling in life than that of seeing the whole Bible as a unified story of God's gracious acts of redemption, and indeed of seeing the whole Bible as ultimately about Jesus, as he himself testified (Luke 24:27; John 5:39).

The ultimate goal of Short Studies in Biblical Theology is to magnify the Savior and to build up his church—magnifying the Savior through showing how the whole Bible points to him and his gracious rescue of helpless sinners; and building up the church by strengthening believers in their grasp of these life-giving truths.

Dane C. Ortlund and Miles V. Van Pelt

Preface

Marriage is not a human invention; it is a divine revelation. Its design never was our own made-up arrangement of infinite malleability. It was given to us, at the beginning of all things, as a brightly shining fixity of eternal significance. We might not always live up to its true grandeur. None of us does so perfectly. But we have no right to redefine it, and we have every reason to revere it.

Only the Bible imparts to us a vision of marriage so transcendent and glorious, far beyond human variation and even human failure. Marriage is of God and reveals a wonderful truth about God. And we have no right to change the face of God in the world. All we can rightly do is receive what God has revealed with gladness and humility.

This is a book about the biblical view of marriage. But that does not mean this book limits its interest to the roles of husbands and wives. That is a valid consideration, and many books have been written about it. But what I mean by "the biblical view of marriage" lifts our thoughts far above even urgently important questions being debated today. The Bible has its eye primarily on the ultimate marriage between the Son of God and his redeemed bride. That eternal romance is the biblical view of marriage, offering both instruction and hope for our own marriages today.

The classical Christian understanding of human marriage was long accepted throughout Western civilization. The traditional wedding service of the Book of Common Prayer, for example, begins:

> Dearly beloved, we are gathered together here in the sight of God, and in the face of this company, to join together this Man and this Woman in holy Matrimony; which is an honorable estate, instituted of God, signifying unto us the mystical union that is betwixt Christ and his Church; which holy estate Christ adorned and beautified with his presence and first miracle that he wrought in Cana of Galilee, and is commended of Saint Paul to be honorable among all men; and therefore is not by any to be entered into unadvisedly or lightly; but reverently, discreetly, advisedly, soberly, and in the fear of God.

But now we are told that this God-centered vision of marriage is mistaken, and worse than mistaken, even oppressive. Now we are told that we will never be a free and just society unless everyone, arranging their sexuality however they wish, may demand formal validation from the state and therefore from us all. Overlook the fact that no class or group has been denied marriage, as it has been understood within the long-held consensus—one man with one woman. That was not withheld, so no one was being discriminated against. But now our collective better future requires civil rights status for the infinite spin-off redefinitions of marriage as baseline civility expected of us all, and failure to comply with the new order is a punishable bigotry.

Clearly we all have the freedom to do what we choose with our own God-given humanity. But we do not have the freedom to escape the consequences of our choices, nor may we rightly demand that others support our choices. As our society departs increasingly from the ways of God, more misery will deeply injure and depress human experience. May the Christian church be ready always to care for sinners and sufferers without a self-righteous "I told you so." May we who follow Christ receive all penitents with tenderness and practical helps. But we need more than an emergency room for people wounded by the sexual revolution. We also need a widespread return to the ancient wisdom we all have foolishly disobeyed.

I wrote this book with two yearnings in my heart. First, I yearn for a recovery of joyful confidence in marriage as God originally gave it to us. This requires a humble, thoughtful return to biblical teachings. We will never see human sexuality restored without a rediscovery of Scripture as the consensus of our culture. Second, I yearn for more men and women to experience enduring marital romance. We will never live in the human richness we all desire without our hearts strengthened by divine grace. So I am sending this book into the world as one more effort in my lifelong desire for reformation and revival in our generation. Reformation is the recovery of biblical truth in its redemptive claim on the whole of life. Revival is the renewal of human flourishing by the Holy Spirit according to the gospel. Marriage is one of the primary flashpoints of controversy where we most need both reformation and revival in our times.

My pledge to you, the reader, is that I will try to stay true to the Bible throughout this book. I want to lead you on a brief journey of discovery from the beginning of the Bible to its end, because the Bible is a love story. It is not a hodgepodge of religious thoughts. The Bible unfolds as a complex but coherent narrative of God gathering a bride for his Son—and he found her on the wrong side of town, too. What a story!

My request of you, the reader, is simply that you will stay open to the surprising things the Bible says about marriage. Our willingness to moderate our personal reactions long enough to keep tracking with the Bible until the story is fully told will be rewarded with satisfying new insights. So why not listen to the story as if for the first time?

Finally, I thank Dane Ortlund and Miles Van Pelt for the privilege of contributing this volume to their series, Short Studies in Biblical Theology. I thank my friends at Crossway for their expert assistance. I thank the elders and members of Immanuel Church, Nashville, for their prayers and partnership. And I thank my wife, Jani, for her sacrificial patience and support while I wrote this book.

May the Lamb receive the reward of his suffering!

1

Marriage in Genesis

If the Bible is telling us the truth about reality, then we have a way to account for the whole of our human experience—both our grandeur and our squalor. The Bible explains both at a radical level. All our personal stories, with both our glory and our shame, began in the garden of Eden. We are all rooted that deeply. The book of Genesis gives us the categories we need if we are going to understand how we went so wrong and whether we have any future worth living for. I agree with Francis Schaeffer:

> In some ways these chapters [in Genesis] are the most important ones in the Bible, for they put man in his cosmic setting and show him his peculiar uniqueness. They explain man's wonder and yet his flaw.[1]

We have good reason, therefore, to consider carefully the early insights of Genesis into ourselves in general and marriage in particular.

---

1. Francis A. Schaeffer, *Genesis in Space and Time: The Flow of Biblical History* (Downers Grove, IL: InterVarsity Press, 1972), 9.

Genesis 1

The biblical love story begins on a grand scale: "In the beginning, God created the heavens and the earth" (Gen. 1:1). The story ends on an even grander scale: "Then I saw a new heaven and a new earth, for the first heaven and the first earth had passed away" (Rev. 21:1). The first cosmos was created as the home of a young couple named Adam and Eve. The new cosmos will be created as the eternal home of the Son and his bride. It is not as though marriage is just one theme among others in the Bible. Instead, marriage is the wraparound concept for the entire Bible, within which the other themes find their places. And if the Bible is telling a story of married romance, no wonder that the demonic powers would forbid marriage (1 Tim. 4:1–5). Every happy marriage whispers their doom and proclaims Christ's triumph.

Grandeur sets the tone of the first creation in Genesis 1. God speaks, and light springs into existence out of nothing but vast darkness. God speaks into reality, into shape and fullness and color and life, both heaven and earth, lands and seas, plants and animals. As the creation account concludes, a new universe sparkles through God's creative word. But the whole would have been incomplete without this climactic act of divine goodness:

> Then God said, "Let us make man in our image, after our likeness. And let them have dominion over the fish of the sea and over the birds of the heavens and over the livestock and over all the earth and over every creeping thing that creeps on the earth."
>
> So God created man in his own image,
> > in the image of God he created him;
> > male and female he created them.

And God blessed them. And God said to them, "Be fruit-
ful and multiply and fill the earth and subdue it, and have
dominion over the fish of the sea and over the birds of the
heavens and over every living thing that moves on the earth."
(Gen. 1:26–28)

The Genesis account of human origins dignifies us all. In the ancient Babylonian creation story, man is degraded. The god Marduk
addresses his father Ea:

Blood I will mass and cause bones to be,
I will establish a savage, "man" shall be his name.
Verily, savage-man I will create.
He shall be charged with the service of the gods
　　That they might be at ease![2]

As the lackey of minor gods who are discontented with their
lot, man exists to perform their menial tasks for them "that they
might be at ease." But in the biblical vision, man is lifted into both
royal activity (Gen. 1:26–28) and Sabbath rest (Gen. 2:1–3; Ex.
20:8–11).

Genesis 1:26–28 makes three assertions about humanity. *First,
God created man as uniquely qualified to rule over his creation.* In
verse 26, "Let us make man in our image, after our likeness" means
that God made us for the exalted purpose of representing him. We
are images of God—but not in a literal, physical way, as little statues
of God. God is spirit, not limited by a body (Deut. 4:12; John 4:24).
So God has no edges, no bulk. But we do image God in that we
were created to stand for God and to advance his purposes here in
his world:

2. James B. Pritchard, ed., *Ancient Near Eastern Texts Relating to the Old Testament* (Princeton, NJ: Princeton University Press, 1969), 68.

Just as powerful earthly kings, to indicate their claim to dominion, erect an image of themselves in the provinces of
their empire where they do not personally appear, so man
is placed upon earth in God's image as God's sovereign
emblem.[3]

The animals are to be identified "according to their kinds" (Gen.
1:21, 24–25). But mankind, and mankind alone, stands tall as royalty
"in the image of God." We find our identity not downward in relation to the creation but upward in relation to God. And the glory
of the divine image extends to every one of us: "In ancient Near
Eastern texts only the king is in the image of God. But in the Hebrew
perspective this is democratized to all humanity."[4] All mankind,
equally together, was created for the high and holy purpose of bringing the glorious rule of God into the world.

Second, God created man in the dual modality of male and female.
Verse 27 is the first poetry in the Bible, rhapsodizing on God's creation of mankind. And the verse's joy comes to a focal point here:
"*male and female* he created them." Nowhere else does the creation
account of Genesis 1 refer explicitly to sexuality. Animal reproduc-
tion is *assumed*, but human sexuality is *celebrated*, though its deeper
meaning is not yet explained. The Babylonian version of creation
does not even mention the creation of the two sexes, but the Genesis
account glories in "male and female he created them." To Genesis
and to Jesus, it was highly meaningful that "he who created them
from the beginning made them male and female" (Matt. 19:4). The
rest of the Bible will explain that meaning with increasing clarity,
taking us into the very heart of the story.

Third, God created man under divine blessing, actively promoting

3. Gerhard von Rad, *Genesis: A Commentary* (Philadelphia: Westminster Press, 1972), 60.
4. Bruce K. Waltke, *Genesis: A Commentary* (Grand Rapids, MI: Zondervan, 2001), 66.

man's glorious destiny. The introductory "And God blessed them," heading verse 28, covers all that God declares in the rest of the verse about humanity fruitfully multiplying and universally ruling. In verse 22, God spoke blessing out over the lower creation: "And God blessed them, saying . . ." But here in verse 28, God speaks his blessing *to us* personally and directly: "And God blessed them. And God said *to them* . . . ," authorizing both male and female to rule, to develop successful human cultures, to leave a mark on the world for the glory of God, all under the smile of God's blessing.

To sum up: Genesis 1 presents the newly fashioned world in its pristine beauty, with mankind as male and female, robed in royal dignity, together stewarding God's wondrous creation for the display of his glory. The Old Testament asserts the greatness of the trust we received: "The earth he has given to the children of man" (Ps. 115:16). The first claim of the Bible, then, setting the stage for marriage, is that manhood and womanhood are not our own cultural constructs. Human concepts are too small and artificial a context for the glory of our sexuality. Manhood and womanhood find their true meaning in the context of nothing less than the heavens and the earth, the cosmos, the universe, the entire creation. That is the first claim of the biblical love story.

Now, if we were reading the Bible for the first time, what question might we ask, as Genesis 1 concludes? Turning the page to chapter 2, we might wonder what kind of sequel could match or exceed the glories of the first chapter. But, in fact, what happens next in the biblical story? After the heavens and the earth come together in the first creation, a man and a woman come together in the first marriage. Surprisingly, the Bible moves from cosmic majesty in Genesis 1 to a common everyday reality in Genesis 2: a young couple falling in love. So we might wonder if marriage is out of its depth here alongside the creation of the universe. Or could it be that the Bible sees in marriage more than we typically do? For now, we will put that question on hold, as we attend first to what Genesis 2:15–25 clearly teaches about marriage.

Genesis 2

The Lord God took the man and put him in the garden of Eden to work it and keep it. And the Lord God commanded the man, saying, "You may surely eat of every tree of the garden, but of the tree of the knowledge of good and evil you shall not eat, for in the day that you eat of it you shall surely die." (Gen. 2:15–17)

Now the Bible's range of vision narrows to a localized focal point: the garden of Eden, where the "male and female" of Genesis 1:27 appear as Adam and Eve.[5] As for Adam, on the one hand, we can see here that he was not a caveman. Verses 15–17 show that his world was not crude and primitive. God put him in an environment rich with potential, available for enjoyment and worthy of his thoughtful effort. God's first commandment, emphatically stated, was strikingly open and generous, in keeping with Adam's royal status over the lower creation: "You may surely eat of every tree of the garden." But on the other hand, Adam was not a god. God defined him as responsible to his Creator. Adam was charged by God to develop the garden—"to work it," presumably until the entire world would grow to become an Edenic kingdom of God's glory. Moreover, Adam was to guard the garden from all evil: ". . . and keep it." That Hebrew verb reappears in Genesis 3:24: ". . . to *guard* the way to the tree of life." God did not explain what kind of threats evil and death are.

---

5. Adam does not name his wife "Eve" until Gen. 3:20, but we will allow ourselves to use her name now for our own convenience.

Rather, the divine warning stands in verse 15 "like a door whose name announces only what lies beyond it,"[6] so that Adam had to obey God's command as a matter of trust. Adam's role was to assert and enjoy his sovereignty under God, cultivating the garden into an expanding paradise and protecting it from all harm.

But, surprisingly, in this Eden of rich resources and splendid potential, in this paradise unharmed by evil and death, God puts his finger on something that is wrong:

> Then the LORD God said, "It is not good that the man should be alone; I will make him a helper fit for him." Now out of the ground the LORD God had formed every beast of the field and every bird of the heavens and brought them to the man to see what he would call them. And whatever the man called every living creature, that was its name. The man gave names to all livestock and to the birds of the heavens and to every beast of the field. But for Adam there was not found a helper fit for him. So the LORD God caused a deep sleep to fall upon the man and, while he slept, took one of his ribs and closed up its place with flesh. And the rib that the LORD God had taken from the man he made into a woman and brought her to the man. Then the man said,
>
> > "This at last is bone of my bones
> >   and flesh of my flesh;
> > she shall be called Woman,
> >   because she was taken out of Man."
>
> Therefore a man shall leave his father and his mother and hold fast to his wife, and they shall become one flesh. And

---

6. Derek Kidner, *Genesis: An Introduction and Commentary* (Downers Grove, IL: InterVarsity Press, 1967), 63.

the man and his wife were both naked and were not ashamed. (Gen. 2:18–25)

Out of something "not good," God creates something very good. This is how the Bible begins to explain the meaning of marriage. God's assessment in verse 18, "It is not good that the man should be alone," is not what we expect in the perfect garden. But his assertion is blunt. "Not good" is stronger in force than a neutral lack of goodness; "not good" is emphatic, definitely bad, a minus factor.[7] But how could it be otherwise? "Love is God's nature, a fundamental characterization of his Trinitarian being."[8] The Bible helps us see that we live in a universe where ultimate reality is relational. For this man to be alone in a world created and ruled by the God who is love—the very fact that it *is* a perfect world makes his aloneness unthinkable. Therefore, God says, "I will make him a helper fit for him."

"A helper fit for him" is a delicately nuanced, two-sided statement about the man and the woman as originally created by God. On the one hand, the woman is the man's helper. But the word *helper* cannot imply inferiority, for God himself is our helper: "Behold, God is my helper; the Lord is the upholder of my life" (Ps. 54:4). Nor can the word *helper* suggest dependence, for man and woman are obviously interdependent (1 Cor. 11:11–12). But the word *helper* does cohere with the fact that God created the woman for the man (1 Cor. 11:9). Verse 18 literally says, "I will make *for him* a helper fit for him." The woman was made to complement and support the man and to strengthen his exertions for God in this world. The man needed a companion like himself, and yet unlike himself, as the friend and ally he could absolutely depend on. The woman completed the man,

---

7. See Umberto Cassuto, *A Commentary on the Book of Genesis: Part I* (Jerusalem: Magnes Press, 1972), 126–27.

8. John M. Frame, *The Doctrine of God* (Phillipsburg, NJ: P&R, 2002), 416.

and he knew it, for he greeted her with relief: "This at last is bone of my bones and flesh of my flesh" (Gen. 2:23). The New Testament will go on clearly to name the man as "head" (1 Cor. 11:3). But his impact for God would be diminished if he were to remain alone without the strong help of a strong woman. He needed her high-capacity contribution. Unified as head and helper, the man and the woman together can prosper as noble servants of their Creator.

The insight offered here by the Bible is bold. It is saying that the delicate interplay between male head and female helper is not a mutation in human social evolution, to be replaced by later developments; it is a stroke of divine genius, original to our existence. Rightly understood and beautifully lived out, God's wise creation of head with helper is a permanent and glorious reality, not arbitrary or eccentric but traceable even up into ultimacy: "The head of every man is Christ, the head of a wife is her husband, and the head of Christ is God" (1 Cor. 11:3). Headship did not come down to us historically as an artifact of oppressive patriarchy; it began in heaven and came down into this world creationally as a pathway to human flourishing. The evils of domination and slavery we invented (Ex. 1:13; 2:23). But the head-with-helper dance of complementarity sprang from deep within the intuitions of God himself. We men and women today do not automatically know the steps to this dance. We must learn. But if we will receive it by faith, trusting in the goodness and wisdom of God, we can then explore its potentialities for joyful human magnificence.

At our moment in time and culture, far advanced in the downward slide of Adam's fall, we today might find the head-with-helper arrangement between husband and wife incomprehensibly foreign. We might desire to replace it with strict mutuality, as if man and woman were interchangeable. But a forced blending of gender identities and roles tends toward a more calculating, hair-splitting, political settlement. Biblical complementarity is the arrangement most conducive to being swept away into a wildly glorious romance. Moreover, before we give up on God's design as unworkable, we must understand that all aspects of manhood and womanhood, with marriage and sex and intimacy—these now fragile glories of human existence, were not created for this broken world. They were created for a perfect world, a safe world, far from our own, and are now brutalized and vandalized, partly by being misjudged. My iPhone, for example, is amazing communications technology. And that is what human sexuality is—amazingly sophisticated communications technology. But if I use my iPhone to hammer nails, I will damage it. It was never built to hammer nails. It was built for something far more gentle, and the more effective for being gentle. The only arrangement for sex and marriage that has any chance of working today is that which moves toward restoring our Edenic origins. If we modern Western egalitarians can hold our emotional horses long enough to imagine how a woman might be dignified by helping a worthy man who loves her sacrificially, as both the man and the woman humbly pursue the glory of God together, the profile of man and woman that blessed us in Eden will start looking more plausible as an approach to human happiness today.

On the other hand, "a helper fit for him" asserts the equal worth of the woman. She is *fit for him*, that is, corresponding to him, on his level, eye-to-eye as his equal, since both equally bear the divine image. The woman is not the man's property or prize of war or political pawn or even, yet, the mother of his children. The woman matters in her own right as the man's unique counterpart, the only one in all the creation who corresponds to him. The man and the woman need and benefit from each other mutually. Their gifts and abilities differ, even widely, but to the advantage of both. The totality of each one's full potential nets out as equal with the other in its capacity to reflect the glory of God, the man in his own way, the woman in her own way. Therefore, between the man and the woman as created by God, personal worth is not stratified to the diminishing of either. Sam Andreades articulates a biblical understanding with wise nuance:

> Gender comes in specialties. Specialties are things we all might do sometimes, but the specialist focuses on especially doing them. We may do many things for each other that are the same, but the gender magic happens when we lean into the asymmetries. Just as, physically, both males and females need both androgen and estrogen hormones, and it is the relative amounts that differ in the sexes, so the gender distinctives are things that both men and women may be able to do, and *do* do, but when done as specialties to one another, they propel relationship.[9]

When we trust God enough to accept his account of manhood and womanhood, the relational quality of our marriages today can open up to deeper possibilities than we could ever create out of our own personal or cultural narratives.

The story unfolding in Genesis 2:18–25 takes another surprising turn when God does not immediately create this helper fit for Adam. Instead, God parades the animals before the man for him to name them. And we know, from his final act of naming in verse 23, that Adam was not slapping an arbitrary label on each animal but observing it thoughtfully and identifying it meaningfully. But why did God put Adam to this task before providing Eve? Because God

---

9. Sam A. Andreades, *enGendered: God's Gift of Gender Difference in Relationship* (Wooster, OH: Weaver, 2015), 132; emphasis original.

wanted to prepare the man, awakening his sense of need, lest God's precious gift be squandered on an uncomprehending and ungrateful man. The not-good aloneness that God perceived, in verse 18, Adam himself did not yet sense. So the thoughtful discovery involved in naming the animals is how God alerts the man to his isolation amid the beauty and plenty of an otherwise perfect world. In fact, verse 20 can be literally translated, "But as for Adam, *he* did not find a helper fit for him." The man now *feels* his isolation and is prepared for the greatest gift, under God, he will ever receive, greater than all the creation itself.

The biblical story now becomes lovingly tender. Verses 21 and 22 suggest the following scene. We can imagine God saying to the man, "Son, I want you to lie down here. That's right. Now, just go to sleep. I want to bless you with a friend such as you cannot imagine. These animals are interesting. But I have a new and better companion in mind for you. But you must rest." Adam falls into a deep sleep. God then opens his side, takes out a rib with its flesh, closes and heals the wound, and creates the woman. She is not refined from the dust of the ground, as was Adam (Gen. 2:7). She comes from Adam himself, doubly refined. Like Jesus multiplying the loaves and fish (Matt. 14:13–21), God the Creator increases the very bone and flesh of the man to build the first woman. As Matthew Henry commented centuries ago, the woman was "not made out of his head to rule over him, nor out of his feet to be trampled upon by him, but out of his side to be equal with him, under his arm to be protected, and near his heart to be beloved."[10] There she stands, the first woman—pure, lovely, dear to God.

So God bends down, touches the man, and says, "Son, you can wake up now. I have one more creature for you to name. I'm very

---

10. Matthew Henry, *Commentary on the Whole Bible* (McLean, VA: MacDonald, n.d.), 1:20.

interested to see your response to this one." And like the father of the bride, God "brought her to the man," according to verse 22. And for the man, it is a case of love at first sight. In verse 23, he rejoices over the woman with the first recorded human words, and they are poetry, moved by love:

> This at last is bone of my bones
> and flesh of my flesh . . .

The man is not threatened by the woman's obvious equality with him. That heartwarming reality is the very thing that pleases him. With relief ("at last"), he greets her as his unique counterpart within the whole of creation. He intuitively identifies with her. His heart is drawn toward her. He prizes her. He rejoices over her. He praises God for her. And in thanking God for her, he perceives her as intimate with himself:

> . . . she shall be called Woman,
> because she was taken out of Man.

With his last act as duly authorized namer in the garden, the man identifies himself and the woman as of one kind, yet distinct from each other. The ultimate human relationship is presented to us as a complementarity of differences, not a duplication of sameness. To quote N. T. Wright in a recent interview on the definition of marriage:

> If you believe in what it says in Genesis 1 about God making heaven and earth—and the binaries in Genesis are so important—heaven and earth, and sea and dry land, and so on, and you end up with male and female. It's all about God making complementary pairs, which are meant to work together. The last scene in the Bible is the new heaven and the new earth

and . . . the marriage of Christ and his church. It's not just one or two verses here and there which say this or that. It's an entire narrative which works with this complementarity, so that a male-plus-female marriage is a signpost or a signal about the goodness of the original creation and God's intention for the eventual new heavens and new earth.[11]

Faithful Christians, married and single, will join with the Bible in its celebration of human complementarity from original creation to eternal destiny by the hand of a wise and good Creator. At the same time, faithful Christians will have serious reservations about the symmetry of sexual sameness. This twofold conviction sets the Christian worldview apart, and that is nothing new. For example, in the introduction to a standard edition of Plato's *Symposium*, the translators write, "It is, actually, a remarkable fact that the *Symposium*, the first explicit discussion of love in western literature and philosophy, begins with a discussion of homosexual love."[12] Since antiquity, the Bible has been speaking a prophetic word into the long-standing sexual confusion of our post-Eden world.

How then does the Bible define marriage? Genesis 2:24 provides the answer. This verse declares the ongoing relevance of the original creation of man and woman. At the fall of Adam in Genesis 3, we did not lose everything of Eden. We still retain, even in our broken world of today, the privilege of marriage. That is what Genesis 2:24 explains:

> Therefore a man shall leave his father and his mother and hold fast to his wife, and they shall become one flesh.

---

11. http://www.firstthings.com/blogs/firstthoughts/2014/06/n-t-wrights-argument-against-same-sex-marriage.

12. Alexander Nehamas and Paul Woodruff, *Plato: Symposium* (Indianapolis: Hackett, 1989), *xiv*.

It is not true that the Bible endorses multiple forms of marriage, and therefore that the Bible fails to provide one clear definition of marriage. The Bible does record, for example, that "Lamech took two wives" (Gen. 4:19). But that biblical statement does not validate polygamy. Nowhere does the Bible's mere mention of a practice amount to approval of that practice. Indeed, Genesis 4:19 is casting doubt on polygamy. The role of Lamech in the Genesis narrative is to show "a progressive hardening in sin."[13] We invented polygamy as a distortion of marriage; but marriage, as created and blessed by God, is defined in Genesis 2:24. What then is this monumental verse saying?

"Therefore." This word signals that Moses is drawing an inference from the Eden narrative for our lives in the world today. It's as if we are sitting in Moses's living room, watching his DVD of the creation of the universe (Genesis 1) and of man and woman (Genesis 2). At this point in the DVD, he hits the pause button on the remote, the screen freezes, he turns to us post-fall people watching these amazing primeval events, and he says to us, "I want you to know how God's original design remains normative for us today. Every marriage now should follow the precedent of God's pattern established back then."

"*. . . a man shall leave his father and his mother.*" If even parental claims must yield to the primacy of marriage, so must all other bonds, however strong. A man's primary human relationship should be with his wife alone, as they start a new family together. In a culture that venerated ancestral ties, this was a radical departure from custom and expectation. And it is not the woman who makes all the sacrifices to get the marriage going. "*A man* shall leave his father and his mother.*"

---

13. Waltke, *Genesis*, 100.

"*. . . and hold fast to his wife.*" The Hebrew root translated "hold fast" is used elsewhere for soldering two parts of metal together (Isa. 41:7). In marrying, a man joins himself to his wife at a profound level. He does not ask her to move his way, to do all the adjusting toward him. But he takes the initiative to move toward his wife, enfolding her into his heart, bonding with her as with no other human being, not even his children. He *rejoices* to identify with his wife, as Adam did with Eve: "This at last is bone of my bones and flesh of my flesh." At every level of his being, a husband should be wholeheartedly devoted to his wife, loyal to his wife, steadfast toward his wife, as toward no other.

"*. . . and they shall become one flesh.*" "One flesh" is the biblical definition of marriage in two brief but freighted words. This expression names marriage as *one mortal life fully shared.* The word *one* bespeaks a life fully shared, and the word *flesh* suggests the transient mortality of this life (Gen. 6:3; Ps. 78:39). So in the one-flesh union of marriage, all the boundaries between a man and a woman fall away, and the married couple comes together completely, as long as they both shall live. In real terms, two selfish me's start learning to think like one unified us, building a new life together with one total everything: one story, one purpose, one reputation, one bed, one suffering, one budget, one family, and so forth. Marriage removes all barriers and replaces them with a comprehensive oneness. It is this all-encompassing unity that sets marriage apart *as marriage*, more profound than even the most intense friendship. As Girgis, Anderson, and George cogently argue,

> A critical point here is that marriage and ordinary friendship do not simply offer different degrees of the same type of human good, like two checks written in different amounts. Nor are they simply varieties of the same good, like the en-

joyment of a Matisse and the enjoyment of a Van Gogh. Each is its own kind of good, a way of thriving that is different in kind from the other.[14]

Friends have much in common, but wise friends also have boundaries. They do not share *everything*. And there is much good in friendship, limited as it is. But what distinguishes marriage is the all-inclusive scope of its claims upon both the man and the woman. The two become "one flesh"—one mortal life fully shared—with total openness, total access, total solidarity, for the rest of their earthly days.

Here then is the biblical claim. Marriage did not arise from historical forces. It came down by heavenly grace as a permanent good for mankind. God gave it, and God gives it. It was, and it is, his to define. And he did define it in Genesis 2:24 as *one mortal life fully shared between one man and one woman*. This is marriage, according to the Bible, because the whole point of Genesis 2:24 is to define marriage for all time, beyond the garden of Eden. We must admit that by this standard, there is no perfect marriage today. Husbands and wives all fall short of the total abandon, the total trust, the total surrender, entailed in real marriage. But the standard still exists, and we diminish our future if we discard it. Moreover, even our imperfect marriages still bear witness to the glory God originally gave. A less than Edenic marriage is still a true marriage, as defined by God, and worthy of personal devotion and legal protection in the world today.

Genesis 2 concludes with one final brushstroke of beauty. In the demandingly all-encompassing context of biblical marriage we also find our greatest earthly comfort:

---

14. Sherif Girgis, Ryan T. Anderson, and Robert P. George, *What Is Marriage? Man and Woman: A Defense* (New York: Encounter, 2012), 14.

And the man and his wife were both naked and were not ashamed. (v. 25)

After his significant aside in verse 24, Moses takes us readers back again into the garden of Eden. In the closing scene of original human innocence, the man and the woman—not the woman only—are naked, face-to-face in a relationship of complete belonging and total vulnerability, where they experience full acceptance, with no shaming. Even so, a biblical marriage today offers the comfort of being known intimately by another and not embarrassed or ridiculed for any reason, but only welcomed and put at ease and embraced. Married couples still experience this aftertaste of Eden's perfect shalom in their gentle intimacy today.

So Genesis 1 and 2 honor marriage as nothing less than the crowning glory of the creation of the universe. For us modern people who may see marriage as a product of human preference driving social evolution, that is a stunning claim. Moreover, the Genesis account honors marriage as both sacred and safe, where a man and a woman can flourish as nowhere else.

But if marriage occupies this exalted place in human reality, how does the Bible account for the tears and betrayals and injuries—in addition to the sheer boredom—within our own marriages today? We must turn the biblical page to the next scene in the story. Genesis 3 explains why we who marry in happiness and hope get our hearts so deeply broken. Why are there so many among us whose joyous romance dissolved into bitter alienation? It is not as though our sexuality itself is at fault or that falling in love is inherently fraudulent, and it is certainly not the case that God overlooked a flaw in his original design for marriage. Something more profound has gone wrong with us. That is where the biblical story goes next.

Genesis 3

What we find in the biblical narrative now is not only how our first parents, Adam and Eve, unleashed hell into the garden of Eden but also how every married couple since has done the same in their own Eden. Reading this account in Genesis 3, it appears that "the fall"— how we tumbled from our original glory down into our present sin and misery and death—the crucial events of the fall of mankind could have taken place in maybe five minutes. But every marriage is always just five minutes away from disaster. We today keep telling the same story over and over again. We can be oblivious to the true magnitude of our choices, the real issues at stake in our moment-by-moment lives. We realize too late how fateful our steps have been. We therefore turn to Genesis 3 with an awareness—a broken-hearted awareness—that this text is perennial in its relevance. This story has a familiar feel, because we really are present here.

> Now the serpent was more crafty than any other beast of the field that the LORD God had made. (Gen. 3:1a)

The narrative begins with a play on words, invisible in the English text. The Hebrew word translated "naked" in Genesis 2:25— "And the man and his wife were both naked . . ."—and the Hebrew word translated "crafty" here in Genesis 3:1 are similarly formed: ᶜarôm and ᶜarûm. The man and the woman were nude, but the Serpent was shrewd, we might say. And the point is, the object of the Serpent's cunning was the man and woman's marital bliss. It was in marriage, and marriage at its best, marriage at its most delicate and beautiful—it was precisely there that the human race came under brilliantly evil attack and fell into all the miseries of our present condition. Our original sin was not political or economic or philosophical or psychological, valid as those considerations are. Our original and fateful misstep was our catastrophic betrayal of our marital innocence. We must grasp the magnitude of this. If we misunderstand the root cause of all our sufferings, we will never embrace our eventual remedy, no matter how sincere we are. How then does the destruction of marriage unfold in the Genesis narrative?

> He said to the woman, "Did God actually say, 'You shall not eat of any tree in the garden'?" And the woman said to the serpent, "We may eat of the fruit of the trees in the garden, but God said, 'You shall not eat of the fruit of the tree that is in the midst of the garden, neither shall you touch it, lest you die.'" (Gen. 3:1b–3)

The tempter, who is Satan (Rev. 12:9), makes a bold move. He repositions the woman's angle of vision on all of reality by casting doubt on God. What the Serpent understood, and what we modern people tend not to see, is that *everything* in human existence, including marriage, is most deeply a God issue. If God is good, then we should trust him and obey him *in everything*. If God is not good, then we have to find our own way *in everything*. But either way, we cannot think piecemeal. Whatever we may believe or not believe about God, our attitude toward him must be all or nothing. Satan wants God to become nothing to us. He knows that if he can destroy devotion to God in our marriages, then the future of the human race is his, and Bedford Falls will stay Pottersville forever.

God had commanded Adam, "You may surely eat of every tree of the garden" (Gen. 2:16), emphasizing the abundance of his generous provision. But Satan deftly twists God's positive command into an insulting and confining prohibition: "Did God actually say, 'You shall not eat of any tree in the garden'?" He may be speaking with a tone of concern in his voice: "Royal Lady, is it really true what I've heard, that God is refusing to share all this with you and Adam? Didn't God himself pronounce all things good? I don't understand how our loving Creator could impose on you, the nobility of this world, such a limitation. Garden Queen, would you please explain this problem to me?" The woman did not know there was a problem. But the question puts her on the defensive. A new thought enters her mind, a sense of confinement, even of injury. Already the Devil has drawn her into a reconsideration of everything on his own terms.

The woman replies, in effect, "We *are* allowed to eat of these trees. But now that you mention it, there is that one tree in the center of the garden—God said, 'Don't eat from it, and don't even touch it, lest you die.'" We readers can see her worldview changing already. God's strongly generous "You may surely eat" is weakened in her mind to bare permission with "We may eat." And although the Tree of the Knowledge of Good and Evil really was there in the midst of the garden (Gen. 2:9), the Tree of Life was also right there; but the woman does not mention the Tree of Life or, presumably, even notice it. Her mental focus is on the little that is forbidden rather than on the much that is provided. She even enlarges the prohibition by saying that the tree may not be touched, though God had not said that. The confinement she feels is spreading, becoming intolerable, because in a hostile mind limitations grow to a maddening degree. Moreover, God had strongly warned, "You shall surely die." But the woman now softens it to ". . . lest you die." Now that her view of the consequences is less alarming, Satan springs on that very point:

> But the serpent said to the woman, "You will not surely die. For God knows that when you eat of it your eyes will be opened, and you will be like God, knowing good and evil." So when the woman saw that the tree was good for food, and that it was a delight to the eyes, and that the tree was to be

desired to make one wise, she took of its fruit and ate, and she also gave some to her husband who was with her, and he ate. Then the eyes of both were opened, and they knew that they were naked. And they sewed fig leaves together and made themselves loincloths. (Gen. 3:4–7)

The Serpent's open denial of God's warning reveals that his original question in verse 1 was insincere. He knows exactly what God had said. He simply contradicts it: "You will not surely die." With the woman's confidence shaken, the Serpent pretends to let her in on a secret: "God knows that when you eat of it your eyes will be opened, and you will be like God, knowing good and evil." To paraphrase the message, "I hate to tell you this, Royal Lady, but you deserve to know. God is holding out on you, and for good reason. He fears your potential. He knows very well the powers that will be yours if you eat this fruit. He obviously has regrets about creating you and empowering you. It may come as a shock, Honored One, but God has become your enemy. I know this garden seems pleasant enough. But, in fact, it is a giant ploy to hold you back. So don't be fooled. Reach out and seize life on your own terms. After all, don't you and Adam wield sovereign dominion over all this? Shouldn't you two have the right to decide for yourselves what's good and evil, what's beneficial and harmful? How can someone else know that for you? This tree, Noble Lady, is your only chance to achieve your potential. Far from deadly, *this* tree is in fact the tree of life. Don't you see? If you *obey* God, you will surely die!"

It was a lie big enough to reinterpret her entire existence, and to this day it colors how we perceive everything. We think we can and must understand reality from our own freely assumed standpoint. But if God really is the wise and good Creator of Genesis 1 and 2, then any consideration of life that discredits or marginalizes him must be false to him and tilted to our own inevitable disadvantage. What's more, if God is really there, then objectivity from God is simply impossible. John Milbank, taking into account the full Christian revelation, asserts a claim as wise as it is bold:

> In the face of the resurrection it becomes finally impossible to think of our Christian narrative as only "our point of view," our perspective on a world that really exists in a different, "secular" way. There is no independently available "real world" against which we must test our Christian convictions, because these convictions are the most final, and at the same time the most basic, *seeing* of what the world is.[15]

What hung in the balance here at our primal temptation, and what hangs in the balance in every marriage day by day, is not a petty rule about this or that; what really hangs in the balance is nothing less than *what reality is.* Whose narrative are we believing and living by, moment by moment?

Having poisoned the woman's mind about God, Satan falls silent and allows the deception to run its course from there. She seems to forget about him as she stands there fascinated by that tree. When verse 6 says, "So when the woman saw . . . ," it is not as though she had not seen the tree before. But now it seems to her that she had never seen it, or anything like it, before. It captivates her. What is filling her thoughts now?

First, the tree is good for food. Its fruit hangs there, tantalizingly delicious. "It doesn't look deadly to me," she must have thought. Second, the tree is a delight to the eyes, offering aesthetic appeal, inviting deeper experience. Third, the tree is to be desired to make

---

15. John Milbank, *The Word Made Strange: Theology, Language, Culture* (Oxford, UK: Blackwell, 1997), 250; emphasis original.

one wise. She can then be her own judge of truth and right. But good things—truly good things, and good at multiple levels—even good things go bad, if we have to disobey God to get them.

After the carefully laid trap of Satan, the actual act of sin is stated briefly, as a matter of simple fact, without a hint of shock. The woman passes the point of no return without even realizing it: "She took of its fruit and ate." She didn't take it all, just some of it. But what her act says to God about God is titanic.

And where is her husband, Adam, in all of this? The second-person verbs in the dialogue of verses 1–5 are all plural in the Hebrew text. Verse 1, for example, says, "Did God actually say, '*You [plural]* shall not eat of any tree in the garden'?" And in verse 2 the woman refers to herself and her husband with the first-person plural: "*We* may eat of the fruit of the trees in the garden." The Serpent drew Eve into speaking for her husband, and she presumed to do so. The man was relevant to the entire matter, naturally. But God held Adam primarily responsible as Eve's head. When God eventually confronted them both, it was Adam whom God called to account: "But the Lord God called *to the man* and said to him, 'Where are *you [singular]*?' . . . Have *you [singular]* eaten of the tree of which I commanded *you [singular]* not to eat?'" (Gen. 3:9, 11). If God was to be obeyed in his Edenic kingdom, it was Adam whom God held responsible to make sure of it. But as the temptation actually unfolded, verse 6 reveals that Adam was present right there, doing nothing, but then giving in: ". . . and she also gave some to her husband *who was with her*, and he ate." The woman was authorized to exercise dominion with the man (Gen. 1:26–28); but her royalty was never meant to be exercised apart from her husband's headship, any more than apart from God's command. Nor was Adam ever meant to abdicate his responsibility to guard the garden (Gen. 2:15) or to treat God's command with passive detachment (Gen. 2:16–17). In fact, according to verse 17, when God as judge explains Adam's guilt, he says that Adam's sin includes obeying his wife rather than God: "Because you have listened to the voice of your wife and have eaten of the tree of which I commanded you, 'You shall not eat of it,' . . ." That Hebrew construction—"listen to the voice of"—means to obey (Ex. 15:26; Judg. 2:20). So Adam was standing there, watching the evil progress without intervening. By his failure to exercise his headship, by his failure to live out his one-flesh union with his wife, he advanced the evil he could have stopped. It is one thing to be taken in by a lie; it is another to allow that lie to take over.

The wife acting as the head, but not a wise head, and the husband acting as the helper, but not a wise helper—*it was the breakdown of marriage that broke everything*. The greatest glory in the universe (Genesis 1–2) became the greatest tragedy in the world (Genesis 3). And only the greatest love can restore us (Rev. 21:1–5).

The immediate consequence for the man and the woman is a painful new self-awareness: "Then the eyes of both were opened, and they knew that they were naked. And they sewed fig leaves together and made themselves loincloths" (Gen. 3:7). What had been immeasurable comfort (Gen. 2:25) suddenly becomes intolerable pain. They reached for their own autonomous interpretation of good and evil, beneficial and harmful. But far from attaining Godlike enlightenment and control, the man and the woman just feel dirty. And the sadness every reader senses here is that the very nakedness God had given them for intimacy now only exposes their shame.

God had warned Adam, "In the day that you eat of it you shall surely die" (Gen. 2:17). But Adam and Eve do not drop dead right then and there. Why not? The insight Augustine offers is that we can be both dead and alive at the same time, and thus endlessly dying.

When Augustine asks what God meant by his warning, "whether it was death of the soul or of the body or of the whole man or that which is called the second death," he concludes, "We must answer, 'All of them.'" God's threat to Adam "included every kind of death, down to the very last."[16] Guilty shame pierced the human conscience that day with a prophetic cry that cannot be fully silenced, alerting us to emotional and relational death now as a warning against extreme, total death yet to come. We too cover our sadness over with our own self-invented loincloth remedies. We too face an enemy every day—the truth about ourselves—and we cannot bear the sight of it. But God's eventual remedy will prove better than ours, when he clothes his own with eternal glory (2 Cor. 5:4).

The Bible is not saying that the new human consciousness of shame was neurotic or illusory. Quite the opposite: "Then the eyes of both were opened, and they knew . . ." Not all our feelings of disgrace are wise, but what Adam and Eve saw about themselves was real. C. S. Lewis helps us rebuild a part of the wisdom we need when he writes:

> The second cause [of our modern loss of a sense of personal wickedness] is the effect of Psychoanalysis on the public mind, and, in particular, the doctrine of repressions and inhibitions. Whatever these doctrines really mean, the impression they have actually left on most people is that the sense of Shame is a dangerous and mischievous thing. We have labored to overcome that sense of shrinking, that desire to conceal, which either Nature herself or the tradition of almost all mankind has attached to cowardice, unchastity, falsehood, and envy. We are told to "get things out into

---

16. Augustine, *The City of God*, trans. Philip Levine (Cambridge, MA: Harvard University Press, 1966), 13.11–12.

the open," not for the sake of self-humiliation, but on the grounds that these "things" are very natural and we need not be ashamed of them. But unless Christianity is wholly false, the perception of ourselves which we have in moments of shame must be the only true one; and even Pagan society has usually recognized "shamelessness" as the nadir of the soul. . . . A recovery of the old sense of sin is essential to Christianity.[17]

The first step in every marriage back toward an imperfect but real taste of Eden is not to cover our anguish with loincloths of self-approval. That is a false remedy. Our first step is rather to face our failures, deceits, and sins with utter honesty before God and each other. For us all, there is nothing more painful and humiliating than self-awareness. But honestly admitting how wickedly we have mistreated God, that is when our hearts start cracking open to his redemption. That is where God waits for us with open arms. And any marriage, however troubled, can have hope when God enters in.

Adam and Eve hide not only from one another behind their pathetic coverings, but both together are hiding from God:

And they heard the sound of the LORD God walking in the garden in the cool of the day, and the man and his wife hid themselves from the presence of the LORD God among the trees of the garden. But the LORD God called to the man and said to him, "Where are you?" And he said, "I heard the sound of you in the garden, and I was afraid, because I was naked, and I hid myself." He said, "Who told you that you were naked? Have you eaten of the tree of which I commanded you not to eat?" The man said, "The woman whom

---

17. C. S. Lewis, *The Problem of Pain* (New York: Macmillan, 1962), 56–57.

you gave to be with me, she gave me fruit of the tree, and I ate." Then the LORD God said to the woman, "What is this that you have done?" The woman said, "The serpent deceived me, and I ate." (Gen. 3:8–13)

Nothing is more natural in our fallen world today than trying to build a happy marriage on a foundation of God avoidance. But it cannot work. Without peace with God, we inevitably shatter the peace we desire with one another. And the root of it all is deeper than our personal capacity for choice; we are handicapped by this rootedness in the history we all share in Adam and Eve. Their running from God in the garden was the beginning of all broken families that leave God out. Martin Luther comments, "It is the utmost stupidity for us to imagine that our cure lies in flight from God rather than in our return to God, and yet our sinful nature cannot return to God."[18] Nakedness before one another Adam and Eve can manage—in their own ridiculous way. But the presence of the Lord they find too terrifying to face. Clearly, something more than a single misstep has befallen our parents. Their hearts have changed toward God at a profound and permanent level. This human flaw— the way we break out in a rash at the approach of God—our allergy toward God is natural to us now the way a birth defect is natural and unchosen (Ps. 51:5). We chose our way into sin in the garden of Eden, but we cannot choose our way out today. The controlling dynamic now is the human spirit deep within, oscillating between proud autonomy and crippling shame. We see it in Adam and Eve evading God here in the garden, and we see it in the God-hating people screaming to the mountains and rocks at the end of time, "Fall on us and hide us from the face of him who is seated on the

---

18. Jaroslav Pelikan, ed., *Luther's Works: Lectures on Genesis*, vol. 1, *Chapters 1–5* (St. Louis, MO: Concordia, 1958), 174.

throne, and from the wrath of the Lamb" (Rev. 6:16). But the broken who are given a new heart by grace will, in the end, experience God's presence as heavenly: "They will see his face" (Rev. 22:4), and God himself will wipe every tear from their eyes (Rev. 21:4). That redeeming grace begins to appear even now in the garden of Eden. God does not abandon Adam and Eve, though they forsook him.

The Lord pursues Adam first—"Where are you [singular]?"—because the man is the head and therefore bears the primary responsibility. But the fragmenting power of sin is already obvious in his cowardly response: "I was afraid, because I was naked, and I hid myself." How differently it might have gone if Adam had simply owned up: "Father, I have sinned against heaven and before you. I am no longer worthy to be called your son" (Luke 15:21). But Adam shows no awareness of his real moral guilt before God. He is absorbed in his own emotions of whiney self-pity: "I was afraid, because I was naked." Even a lost little boy knows better, when his father finally shows up. But Adam slinks around like a victim, unable to trust God and face himself and comfort his brokenhearted wife: "I hid myself."

But when we resist God's grace, he often presses in with yet more grace, as here in the garden. God graciously, frankly confronts Adam, "Have you eaten of the tree of which I commanded you not to eat?" Although Adam now admits the truth, he shifts the blame to Eve and implies it is God's fault to begin with: "The woman *whom you gave to be with me*, she gave me fruit of the tree, and I ate." In other words, "God, I don't recall ever asking you for this woman. And look what *she's* done." Eve, for her part, can only hang her head in shame: "The serpent deceived me, and I ate."

The deceitfulness of sin is this. Up front, it sparkles with promise. But once we commit, when it is too late to back out, it entangles us in repercussions we did not foresee and consequences we cannot evade. Only God sees the full impact of our fall. Only God can absorb into himself the final penalty of it. And he will, through Jesus Christ. But in the meantime, with three "oracles of destiny,"[19] God redefines the future of Eden, changing from prose to poetry in keeping with the solemnity of the moment. First:

> The LORD God said to the serpent,
> "Because you have done this,
>> cursed are you above all livestock
>> and above all beasts of the field;
> on your belly you shall go,
>> and dust you shall eat
>> all the days of your life.
> I will put enmity between you and the woman,
>> and between your offspring and her offspring;
> he shall bruise your head,
>> and you shall bruise his heel." (Gen. 3:14–15)

God is the only one who speaks. Satan listens in silence as God pronounces his sentence, and there is nothing Satan can do about it. What then is God saying here to the enemy of our love and romance and joy and intimacy and tenderness and every echo of Eden we cherish to this day? Three things. First, Satan is doomed. The word "cursed" (ʿarûr) in verse 14 plays on the word "crafty" (ʾarûm) in verse 1. The Serpent was devious but is now damned. Satan thought he was so clever, but all his works and ways are condemned, because the garden still belongs to God and a great destiny still awaits the man and the woman.

Second, Satan is humiliated. The proud author of "Invictus" vowed he would die defiantly, his head "bloody but unbowed."[20] But

---

19. Kidner, *Genesis*, 71.
20. William Ernest Henley, *Poems* (London: David Nutt, 1919), 119.

God is saying that Satan will not have the satisfaction of going down in defeat with his head held high: "On your belly you shall go" every moment of his wretched existence.

Third, Satan is crushed. Satan declared war on God, he recruited Eve, and she joined him in trying to shove God aside. Now God declares war on Satan. But at the same time, in grace, God declares peace with Eve when he says, "I will put enmity between you and the woman, and between your offspring and her offspring." This takes some explaining.

Augustine helps us understand that God's decree here in the garden is creating two opposing human communities—Augustine calls them "cities"—that will now develop in the course of history:

> Two cities have been formed by two loves: the earthly by the love of self, even to the contempt of God; the heavenly by the love of God, even to the contempt of self. The former, in a word, glories in itself, the latter in the Lord. For the one seeks glory from men; but the greater glory of the other is God, the witness of conscience. The one lifts up its head in its own glory; the other says to its God, "You are my glory, and the lifter up of my head."[21]

Augustine's metaphor of the city is a good one, because Cain, an offspring of the Serpent, built the first city (Gen. 4:17). God created a garden to share his joy with man, but Cain invented the city to shut God out. And in this world, Cain's purpose succeeds. The rest of the Bible tells the story of the offspring of the Serpent dominating human affairs, as insecure fugitives gather together, convinced that this world they control is all that matters. They pool their talents

---

21. Augustine, *The Works of Aurelius Augustine, Bishop of Hippo: The City of God*, ed. and trans. Marcus Dods (Edinburgh: T&T Clark, 1872), 2:49.

to build entire cultures of self-exalting rebellion against God, as if he were our worst nightmare; and their purpose often succeeds. Moreover, that human collectivity, divided in many ways but united against God, also stands opposed to the offspring of the woman (1 John 3:8–15). But the true offspring of the woman are distinguished by newly rehumanized hearts, created by the grace of God. They bow in surrender to him and luxuriate by faith in his promises of a redeemed world only God can build, and will build, in the future (Rev. 21:1–4). This human collectivity is traceable through the biblical narrative of history and culminates in Jesus, the only unfallen man, wounded by the Serpent at the cross but by that very wounding the conqueror of the Serpent. Jesus is nothing less than a second Adam and head of the redeemed human race, who will live forever (1 Cor. 15:22). What God decrees here in the garden, then, is this new reality: by the gentle force of his one-way love, he sets Eve and her offspring apart to himself, creating in them a bitter loathing for Satan and his empty promises and a yearning for God and his glorious promises of the new Adam, through whom they will crush the Serpent (Rom. 16:20).

For us, the first divine oracle gives us an insight into our experience. Not only must every married couple today choose sides in this great conflict tearing human history apart, but we also need God's help to choose wisely. Left to ourselves, we will never stop replaying the drama of the fall in Genesis 3. We will compulsively keep trying to make God avoidance successful, and we will die in that folly and futility, because our wills are no longer free to trust God. We literally need God to put into us enmity and hostility toward Satan, or we will serve our enemy forever.

The second oracle of destiny addresses Eve and all women who follow, in verse 16, while the third addresses Adam and all men who follow, in verses 17–19. We will be better positioned to understand what God is accomplishing by these declarations, if we bear in mind what C. S. Lewis wrote:

> There is something which unites magic and applied science while separating both from the "wisdom" of earlier ages. For the wise men of old the cardinal problem had been how to conform the soul to reality, and the solution had been knowledge, self-discipline, and virtue. For magic and applied science alike the problem is how to subdue reality to the wishes of men: the solution is a technique; and both, in the practice of this technique, are ready to do things hitherto regarded as disgusting and impious.[22]

What God says in verses 16–19 shapes our reality in ways we cannot overrule, no matter how clever our magic or advanced our science. By his massive words in the garden, God our judge confines all of human experience thereafter to enfeebling pain and final death. And wisdom counsels us to bow in deep acceptance and find eternal life right there in our pain, where we least expect it. How we respond personally to God's decrees is filled with consequence. If we hate God for imposing these limits on us, if we strive to re-create reality more to our liking, we will trend not toward freedom and hope but toward disgusting and impious degradations, and there is no depth to which we will not fall even further. But if we humbly bend to the sorrows and buffetings of this life, trusting God, we will be surprised to discover beauty where God has hidden it—not in our fantasies but in his realities. God's wise purpose in these solemn oracles of destiny is to draw us all back to his loving heart. Therefore, as we embrace the brokenness of life, we begin our journey back to

---

22. C. S. Lewis, *The Abolition of Man* (New York: Macmillan, 1973), 87–88.

God and healing. What God says here explains, in particular, the brokenness of sex and marriage throughout history down to the present day. So then, as for the woman:

> To the woman he said,
> "I will surely multiply your pain in childbearing;
>> in pain you shall bring forth children.
> Your desire shall be for your husband,
>> and he shall rule over you." (Gen. 3:16)

Two realities now define the woman's experience. First, as a mother, she will suffer in childbirth. Children are not a death sentence for any woman, but quite the opposite. A mother's influence contributes to God's final victory over all evil and misery through her children, if they go on to serve the Lord in their generation (1 Tim. 2:15). But she does pay a price for her children in many ways. Eve's paradise is marred, but the woman still gives birth to the future of the world.

Second, as a wife, she will clash with her husband. But two questions stand out here. (1) What is the nature of the woman's "desire"? (2) In what sense does the man "rule" over her?[23] Similar language appears in Genesis 4:7, where God warns Cain about his sinful inclinations: "Its *desire* is for you, but you must *rule* over it." Clearly, sin's desire is to control Cain; but his willpower must push back to gain the mastery over sin. The Hebrew wording behind our English version of Genesis 3:16 is similar: "Your desire shall be for your husband, and he shall rule over you." Applying the logic of Genesis 4:7 to our text, then, God is saying that Eve's created role as a helper fit for him will now be distorted into a desire to control Adam. During

---

23. See Susan T. Foh, "What Is the Woman's Desire?," *Westminster Theological Journal* 37 (1974/75): 376–83.

the temptation she stepped into her husband's role of headship, and now that momentary impulse will become a broader pattern. Adam, for his part, will no longer serve and defend the woman with the noble headship God designed for him. Adam will dominate his wife unkindly, even cruelly, for his own selfish gratification and convenience, more a master than a lover, more a critic than an admirer. This is why the New Testament admonishes husbands, "Husbands, love your wives, *and do not be harsh with them*" (Col. 3:19). The point here in Genesis is that the gentle harmony of Eden now dissolves into "the battle of the sexes" infamous throughout history. Our beautiful wedding vow "to love and to cherish" is now shattered by the opposing forces of her grasping desire and his oppressive rule, leading to countless stories of marital heartache. Only the gospel of Jesus can free us from this endless power struggle and restore the romance, the beauty, the joy, the harmony God intended—manly initiative cherishing and defending the woman, womanly support affirming and empowering the man.

Here, then, is the ultimate reason for our broken promises, shouting matches, resentments, abuses, separations, divorces, and all marital tragedies: God gave us up to the powers of our own sinful confusion. These sad words he declared in Genesis 3:16 predict our cycle of dysfunction whenever a wife steps in to fill the void created by her husband's failure to care and provide, with the husband resenting his wife for the implied criticism of his own passivity and silently or aggressively punishing her for it. Each one aggravates the weakness of the other, as they spiral down into mutual incomprehension, bitterness, alienation. Both defiant feminism and arrogant patriarchy fall short of the glory of Eden. And we husbands and wives will never get ourselves back to the garden by pointing an accusing finger at the other. According to the Bible, all restoration begins with merciful redemption coming down from God above. But what we must never forget is this: when we forsook our Father in the garden, it is not as though we offended him only; we jeopardized everything that we ourselves long for in our own deepest intentions. Whenever we walk away from God, we walk toward something inhumane, unsafe, life-depleting. To put it yet another way, the only alternative to heaven is hell. There is no neutral ground of our own making, under our own control. That world exists nowhere.

Women today, and in every age, suffer the losses decreed in Genesis 3:16 in a profound way. A wise husband will understand that his wife bears burdens he may have little awareness of, because they are bound up in the distinct experience of the woman. A wise husband will take care, therefore, to be all the more mindful of her, to listen to her and stand with her as her friend and her ally and her admirer and her defender. No wife should ever feel that she must face life alone. And as for the man:

> And to Adam he said,
> "Because you have listened to the voice of your wife
>   and have eaten of the tree
> of which I commanded you,
>   'You shall not eat of it,'
> cursed is the ground because of you;
>   in pain you shall eat of it all the days of your life;
> thorns and thistles it shall bring forth for you;
>   and you shall eat the plants of the field.
> By the sweat of your face
>   you shall eat bread,
> till you return to the ground,
>   for out of it you were taken;

for you are dust,
>   and to dust you shall return." (Gen. 3:17–19)

The new reality defining the man's experience is not work but the painful futility of work, the inevitable failure of all earthly accomplishments, the illusion of a man making his mark by the power of his own self-exalting glory. When God says, "Cursed is the ground," we can see the fertility and abundance of the entire earth shriveling up as a weed-infested wasteland, where a man must now strain to eke out a living—as long as he can.

The apostle Paul echoes God's word to Adam when he writes, "The creation was subjected to futility" (Rom. 8:20). The writer of Ecclesiastes asserts, "Futility, utter futility . . . everything is futile" (Eccles. 1:2 REB). David sighs, "Man is like a breath; his days are like a passing shadow" (Ps. 144:4). It is painful for a man to work hard and exercise intelligence and seem to gain ground in this life, only to see his carefully assembled empire shattered by a reversal of fortunes or the betrayal of a partner or the hammer blow of death. Woody Allen, in his own way, helps us face the realism of the Bible:

> I always see the death's head lurking. I could be sitting at Madison Square Garden at the most exciting basketball game, and they're cheering and everything is thrilling, and one of the players is doing something very beautiful—and my thought will be, "He's only twenty-eight years old and I only wish he could savor this moment in some way, because this is as good as it's going to get for him." . . . The fundamental thing behind all motivation and all activity is the constant struggle against annihilation and against death. It's absolutely stupefying in its terror, and it renders anyone's accomplishments meaningless. As Camus wrote, it's not only

that he dies or that man dies but that you struggle to do a work of art that will last and then realize that the universe itself is not going to exist after a time.[24]

One reason we can trust the Bible is its honesty about our lot in life. It is simply undeniable that no amount of diligence or intelligence or even luck can lift us above the overwhelming powers of futility in this broken world. Our careers and degrees and club memberships and civic awards are so many sand castles on the beach, which the waves of time wash over, and soon we are utterly forgotten. This reality is hard to bear. It is hard precisely because we were created in God's image to stride through this world with lasting impact for his eternal glory. But now we are dust, and to dust we shall return. It wears a man down. It wears a married couple down. Many marriages, even if they stay together, just lose their sparkle under the crushing weight of the sheer exhaustions of this life. A wise husband faces his disillusionment, humbly confessing his fears and his needs to his wife. Then the two of them together can take these sorrows to God in prayer and find a hope beyond the curse. Or a man can live in denial—until he can't.

Adam, wisely, gave up early and found in the promises of God a hope this world cannot give and cannot destroy:

The man called his wife's name Eve, because she was the mother of all living. And the LORD God made for Adam and for his wife garments of skins and clothed them. Then the LORD God said, "Behold, the man has become like one of us in knowing good and evil. Now, lest he reach out his hand and take also of the tree of life and eat, and live forever—" therefore the LORD God sent him out from the

---

24. F. Rich, "Woody Allen Wipes the Smile off his Face," *Esquire*, May 1977, 75–76.

garden of Eden to work the ground from which he was taken. He drove out the man, and at the east of the garden of Eden he placed the cherubim and a flaming sword that turned every way to guard the way to the tree of life. (Gen. 3:20–24)

God's promise that the offspring of the woman will come and crush the Serpent once and for all breathes hope into Adam's heart. Adam knows by now that he is not the savior of the world. He has destroyed the world (Rom. 5:12). But a true victor is coming. And he will not just offset evil; much more, he will reign with superabounding grace toward the undeserving (Rom. 5:15–21). Therefore, Adam turns back to his wife not with hypocritical blaming, as in verse 12, but to rejoice over the greatness of her destiny in the redemptive purpose of God. He honors her now as Eve, the Living One and the mother of all those who truly live.[25] The future of the human race is not death only but also life, real and eternal life pulsing in the hearts of all who cherish God's promise as their only hope. True believers are truly living. And Adam sees his wife, Eve, who also believes God's promise, as the spiritual mother of this endless line of believers yet to come. His belief in God softens his heart toward his wife. Before she changes in any noticeable way, and only because God has made them a promise, Adam starts setting a new tone of hope and healing in their marriage. It is the gospel that renews a broken marriage.

We husbands and wives today can see ourselves here, as Adam and Eve turn to leave the garden. We too are exiles from Eden. But whatever we may suffer as we await the renewal of all things, the promises of God can outperform the amusements and even the

---

25. The margin of the ESV comments, "*Eve* sounds like the Hebrew for *life-giver* and resembles the word for *living.*"

therapies of this world in keeping our souls and our marriages alive. The key to a lasting romance is not endless sex but believing hearts. God has given us a wonderful promise of restoration by his grace. We most certainly will get back to the garden someday, led by one who through his suffering opened the way for Adam and Eve and us and millions more (Rev. 22:1–5).

The most remarkable thing about marriage today is not that it can be troubled but that we still have this privilege at all. When God justly expelled us from the garden of Eden, he did not take this gift back. He let us keep his priceless gift, though we sometimes misuse it. But what every married couple needs to know is that their marriage is a remnant of Eden. This is why every marriage is worth working at, worth fighting for. A marriage filled with hope in God is nothing less than an afterglow of the garden of Eden, radiant with hope until perfection is finally restored.

Whatever else the Bible has to say about marriage—and it has much to say—the sadness of Genesis 3 will linger, and so it should. Jonathan Edwards, in *The Religious Affections*, counsels us to accept, along with the joyful hope of the gospel, the tender sadness as well. The sadness saves us from being glib and shallow and pushy and proud. The sadness cracks our hearts open to the deeper things of God. Edwards wrote:

> All gracious affections that are a sweet odor to Christ, and that fill the soul of a Christian with a heavenly sweetness and fragrance, are broken-hearted affections. A truly Christian love, either to God or men, is a humble broken-hearted love. The desires of the saints, however earnest, are humble desires. Their hope is a humble hope; and their joy, even when it is unspeakable and full of glory, is a humble broken-hearted joy, and leaves the Christian more poor in spirit,

and more like a little child, and more disposed to a universal lowliness of behavior.[26]

To sum up, our primary takeaway from the book of Genesis is both the glory of marriage and the brokenness of marriage. The glory is built in by God: the one-flesh union of man and woman. The brokenness is what every generation keeps inheriting from Adam in his original sin, which we then keep making still worse. But the glory purposed by God will have the final say.

His love story has only begun.

---

26. Jonathan Edwards, *The Religious Affections* (Edinburgh: Banner of Truth, 1997), 266.

2

Marriage in the Law, Wisdom, and Prophets

The narratives of Genesis, after chapter 3, include many scenes of married life, with human follies galore, including the bizarre (Gen. 29:31–30:24). These less than exemplary marriages leave us rolling our eyes. It did not take the people of God long to drift far from Eden. But how could it otherwise? The people God draws to himself are sinners. God seems to be attracted to the most hopeless cases. So as we read the Genesis accounts of Abraham and Sarah, Isaac and Rebekah, Jacob and Leah and Rachel, we intuitively make allowances for the eyebrow-raising episodes in their lives. What the Bible records, it does not always condone.

The Law

The law of Moses is another matter. The law commands. That is the point. And many of these ancient laws are obviously admirable. For example, Deuteronomy 24:5 commands, "When a man is newly married, he shall not go out with the army or be liable for any other public duty. He shall be free at home one year to be happy with his wife whom he has taken." The last clause there, "whom he has taken," does not imply force. It restates the intimacy of "and hold fast to his wife" in Genesis 2:24. The emphasis of the law is on the exemption a man should be given from military and other forms of compulsory service for the first full year of married life, "to be happy with his wife." (A similar pronouncement is found in Deut. 20:7.) But this law is even more delightful than it at first appears, for a literal translation of the Hebrew verb yields a richer meaning: "He shall be free at home one year *and shall give happiness to his wife*" (NASB). It is not the husband's happiness that is commanded; it is the wife's happiness, nurtured by the husband.

The context preceding this happy law is a law regulating divorce (Deut. 24:1–4). This foregoing law is intended to prevent frivolous divorces spiraling down into wife-swapping. Then follows this positive law, meant to strengthen the marital bond in its first, foundational year. Not only does Deuteronomy 24:5 guard against a young husband's untimely death in combat, leaving behind a brokenhearted widow, and not only does it prevent his prolonged absence from home so soon after the wedding, but it also requires a husband to devote the first year of his new marriage to gently cheering his wife, as she adjusts to her new life away from her family and the challenges of living with a man. It also gives the couple time for a child to be conceived and perhaps born. According to the law of Moses, then, "Time [for a newly married couple] was a precious thing, too precious to be taken by government even in times of war."[1]

Who today would not appreciate this ancient law? Other laws

---

1. Eugene H. Merrill, *Deuteronomy* (Nashville, TN: Broadman, 1994), 391.

of Moses do not immediately satisfy our moral sensibilities today. I will cite one in a moment. But the concerns we bring to the Mosaic law might be moderated, to some degree, if we realize what God was accomplishing by it. The law of Moses was never meant to define the zenith of human moral grandeur. The Bible itself says that the law was not faultless and that it eventually became obsolete (Heb. 8:7, 13). In its limited capacities, the law failed to uphold the moral standards of God's ancient people, and they fell under the judgment of God. What made the Old Testament legal arrangement between God and his people unsustainable was not a moral flaw in the law itself but something familiar to us all: human weakness.

What the New Testament clarifies is this: within the flow of the Bible as a whole, we should see the law of Moses as something "added" (Gal. 3:19). That is, the law was built into the Bible as a sidebar, temporarily running parallel with the gracious promises of God. The promises come first and define the main plot in the biblical story. The promises, therefore, by taking precedence, define the larger context for understanding everything in the Bible, including the law. And this addition of the law of Moses was valid only until the coming of Jesus, who is himself the final standard and true fulfillment of everything promised and commanded by the Bible from cover to cover. Everything the people of God failed to be and do, Jesus was and did for us all. He, not the law, is the defining center of how God relates to us. So the Bible has a forward tilt built in, with all aspects of the Old Testament leaning toward Christ: "And the Scripture, foreseeing . . ." (Gal. 3:8).

But the law, provisional though it was, made a real contribution. In its historical setting, as God led his people toward the Promised Land in Canaan, trouble awaited them there. Canaanite culture was a moral sewer, and Israel was a dry sponge. So before God threw that sponge into that sewer, he soaked the sponge in the oil of a culture of holiness. He gave Israel their own culture, defined by the books of the law, Exodus through Deuteronomy. By soaking in the laws of purity and diet and sacrifice and worship and all aspects of holiness, the people could be set apart to God and protected from moral pollution in Canaan—in theory, anyway. Sadly, the people did not obey the law. But it had a noble purpose in its time (Ex. 19:5–6).[2]

Then Jesus came. He obeyed God, fulfilling the law thoroughly (Matt. 5:17). In his very person, Jesus embodied the full meaning of both the promises and the laws of the Old Testament. More than anyone else, he qualified as an expert in the law. To cite a marriage-related question he was asked, he taught us how to perceive the divorce law of Deuteronomy 24:1–4. He explained that this law was more a concession to our moral obtuseness than a declaration of the heart of God:

> They said to him, "Why then did Moses command one to give a certificate of divorce and to send her away?" He said to them, "Because of your hardness of heart Moses allowed you to divorce your wives, but from the beginning it was not so." (Matt. 19:7–9)

What his contemporaries perceived as a command, Jesus saw as an allowance. A command calls for moral elevation and should be sought, but an allowance adjusts downward and might be accepted, though reluctantly. Jesus saw the Mosaic law of divorce as a decline from the beauty of "the beginning," that is, the garden of Eden. And he certainly did not say that the origins of marriage in the garden were no longer relevant to our problems today. He saw God's gift in

---

2. I owe the analogy of the sponge and the sewer to Richard F. Lovelace, *Dynamics of Spiritual Life: An Evangelical Theology of Renewal* (Downers Grove, IL: InterVarsity Press, 1979), 184–85.

Eden as the norm to be admired and pursued and protected, and he saw the law of divorce as a tragic concession, a last resort.

Here is the point. Jesus's understanding of the divine intent behind this divorce law repositions us to interpret the entire law with deeper insight. God was not taking highly civilized people who spent their Sunday afternoons reading Shakespeare and singing madrigals and degrading them with the law of the jungle. Instead— with thanks to J. R. R. Tolkien for the imagery—we can think of the law of Moses as God speaking into an orc culture, regulating its worst features as the beginning of a long process of restoring them to their lost elf culture. God does not accomplish this miracle all at once, because the change he has in mind is not a simple matter of polish and manners. God intends to re-create his people from deep within, and then cultivate their behavior in every respect, so that ultimately Mordor is transformed into Lothlórien. This merciful purpose of God runs through stages of time, as the Bible progresses from the lost garden of Eden to the provisional law of Moses to the glorious culmination in Jesus. And God wisely started with his old-covenant people Israel right where they were in history. From there he patiently led them step by step toward the better world he had promised, a world Jesus alone can create.

So then, the striking thing about the laws of the Old Testament is not that some of them are beneath the modern conscience but that they are above the other law codes of the ancient world. As troubling as some Mosaic laws are to us today, in their own time they were a step in the right direction. To quote a scholar in this field, "There is a humanitarian ethos in Israelite penal law, which is acknowledged by all who have compared it with contemporary ancient Near Eastern collections of law."[3]

---

3. Christopher J. H. Wright, *Old Testament Ethics for the People of God* (Downers Grove, IL: InterVarsity Press, 2004), 309.

An example of a Mosaic law which strikes us today as oddly remote and mystifying is the law concerning levirate marriage—from the Latin *levir*, meaning "brother-in-law." The law states:

> If brothers dwell together, and one of them dies and has no son, the wife of the dead man shall not be married outside the family to a stranger. Her husband's brother shall go in to her and take her as his wife and perform the duty of a husband's brother to her. And the first son whom she bears shall succeed to the name of his dead brother, that his name may not be blotted out of Israel. And if the man does not wish to take his brother's wife, then his brother's wife shall go up to the gate to the elders and say, "My husband's brother refuses to perpetuate his brother's name in Israel; he will not perform the duty of a husband's brother to me." Then the elders of his city shall call him and speak to him, and if he persists, saying, "I do not wish to take her," then his brother's wife shall go up to him in the presence of the elders and pull his sandal off his foot and spit in his face. And she shall answer and say, "So shall it be done to the man who does not build up his brother's house." And the name of his house shall be called in Israel, "The house of him who had his sandal pulled off." (Deut. 25:5–10)

The rationale for a levirate marriage is summed up in verse 6: "And the first son whom she bears shall succeed to the name of his dead brother, that his name may not be blotted out of Israel." Preserving and perpetuating family identity mattered because of the long-term hope held out to the people of God in his many promises, beginning with Genesis 3:15, which we have considered. The genealogies of the Old Testament (e.g., Gen. 5:1–32; 10:1–32) carefully, name by name, trace the historical lineage of the people of God as time bears them along toward the promised redemption. Now the levirate law is enacted in order to ensure the legitimate conservation of an Israelite family in its historical journey toward their promised inheritance, though the eventual new creation of resurrection will far transcend the culture of hope that looked forward to it (Matt. 22:23–33). But the brother-in-law who forsakes his family responsibility is declaring not only how little he cares for his relatives but also how lightly he values the promises of God, presumably because of their present, practical, social obligations. In a culture of hope, which is what God's people are always called to be, such a man and his family line were to be publicly stigmatized as nonnormative. But the levirate law could be obeyed with magnificent nobility, as in the case of Boaz, leading to David (Ruth 1:1–4:22) and eventually to Jesus (Matt. 1:5).

Levirate marriage was practiced in other ancient cultures as well, with variations in the legal provisions. But the hope of a promised future was not the pulse beating at the heart of these other levirate laws:

> In the Hittite Laws and most of the Assyrian Laws it is immaterial whether the deceased man left children. The aim of the practice is not to provide him with a son, but to maintain the investment of his father, who had paid a bride-price for the widow, and to provide support for her.[4]

So then, taking into account both its biblical and its historical settings, the law of Moses as a whole is rightly seen as a more hopeful ordering of human life, compared with other ancient law codes, and therefore prepares the way meaningfully for the promised Messiah.

---

4. Jeffrey H. Tigay, *Deuteronomy: The JPS Torah Commentary* (Philadelphia: Jewish Publication Society, 1996), 483.

We should not fault the law of Moses for falling short of the human beauty Jesus alone could create by his death and resurrection. Instead, we should say of the law what Jesus said of the devout woman: "She has done what she could" (Mark 14:8).

One final word about marriage under the law. To quote Old Testament scholar Bruce Waltke, "Though certainly marriage is not required for holiness, it is instructive to observe that the holiest people in the Old Testament are married."[5] For example, the high priest, who alone could enter God's presence, was a married man (Lev. 21:13). And the Nazirites, the most dedicated of the laypeople, were set apart to God by a vow and with carefully defined rules for demonstrating their separateness (Num. 6:1–21). But they could be married, and they did not fast sexually. Under the law, marriage was fully compatible with holiness.

The Wisdom Books

The joyous worldview of Genesis 1 reappears as the foundation of the book of Proverbs. But the biblical proverbs take the cosmic grandeur of the creation account and press it gently down into the details of our ordinary lives today. Wisdom was powerfully present at the creation, "rejoicing in his inhabited world and delighting in the children of man" (Prov. 8:31). So there is nothing petty and small and legalistic about God's wisdom. His ways are how we swim with the current of reality, how we cut with the grain, how we get home by the right road.

Much of the book of Proverbs appears in disconnected short sayings, like fortune cookies, though more profound! But the soundbite nature of the proverbs means we have to group them together

---

5. Bruce K. Waltke, *An Old Testament Theology: An Exegetical, Canonical, and Thematic Approach* (Grand Rapids, MI: Zondervan, 2007), 237.

according to their themes. A major theme appearing here and there in the book is marriage, and especially sex. Two passages fill out further the Old Testament view of marriage.

First, in Proverbs 5, the sage urges married couples strongly toward sexual joy. Speaking with highly figurative language, the wise man counsels a married man this way:

> Drink water from your own cistern,
>> flowing water from your own well.
> Should your springs be scattered abroad,
>> streams of water in the streets?
> Let them be for yourself alone,
>> and not for strangers with you. (Prov. 5:15–17)

The key to understanding the sexual wisdom of Proverbs is to combine both form and freedom, both structure and liberation. Conservative people love form and restraint and control. Progressive people love freedom and openness and choices. Both see part of the truth, but wisdom sees more. Wisdom teaches us that God gave us our sexuality both to focus our romantic joy and to unleash our romantic joy. When our desires are both focused and unleashed—both form and freedom—our sexual experience becomes wonderfully intensified. A marriage can flourish within both form and freedom, because sex is like fire. In the fireplace, it keeps us warm. Outside the fireplace, it burns the house down. This passage in Proverbs 5 is saying, "Keep the fire within the marital fireplace, and stoke that fire as hot as you can."

The Bible's metaphor for sexual satisfaction is the water that can slake a raging thirst: "Drink water from your own cistern, flowing water from your own well." A man brings into his marriage pent-up sexual desires, passions, and powers. And wisdom is saying, "*Satisfy* your thirst through lovemaking with your wife." Wisdom is *not* say-ing, "You feel desire? And there's temptation out there? Then what you need is an iron will. So there's your future—endless frustration bottled up inside." Self-control is an important part of maturity. But wisdom believes that God's remedy for a man's thirst for sex is sex—overflowing sexual joy with his wife: "your own cistern," "your own well." A man's wife is his own personal, divinely approved wellspring of endless sexual satisfaction.

Every Christian married couple may rightly see, by faith, their heavenly Father raising his hands in blessing over their marriage bed. I say that, because the sage adds a prayer: "May your fountain be blessed."[6] He declares a blessing over the married sexual experi-ence of the young man who accepts his counsel:

[May] your fountain be blessed,
>   and rejoice in the wife of your youth,
>   a lovely deer, a graceful doe.
Let her breasts fill you at all times with delight;
>   be intoxicated always in her love. (Prov. 5:18–19)

What does this fountain of divine blessing look like in a mar-riage? Joyously bubbling sexual happiness between husband and wife. Even as the years go by, she will always be "the wife of your youth." A wise husband will always cherish his wife and rejoice over her as that dear girl who once gave herself completely to him alone. The image of a "lovely deer, a graceful doe" is culturally remote from us. But what the author has in mind appears to be "their bright black eyes, their graceful limbs, and their irresistible silky hair."[7] So

---

6. The ESV translates, "Let your fountain be blessed," which is not inaccurate, but it sounds like a mere wish. "May your fountain be blessed," also accurate, is clearer as a benediction.

7. Bruce K. Waltke, *The Book of Proverbs: Chapters 1–15* (Grand Rapids, MI: Eerdmans, 2004), 321.

the sage is proposing an approach to married sexuality at once both happy and practical: "Husband, enjoy your wife visually. Wife, present yourself to your husband attractively." Of all the women on the face of the earth, a man's wife is the one and only morally legitimate satisfaction of his sexual passions.

"Let her breasts fill you at all times with delight; be intoxicated always in her love" emphasizes two things: the *quality* of lovemaking ("fill . . . with delight" and "be intoxicated") and the *quantity* of lovemaking ("at all times" and "always"). The wisdom of God is saying, "When you get married, drop your inhibitions, and *go for it.*" Back in the days of the Puritans, when a New England wife complained, first to her pastor and then to the whole congregation, that her husband was neglecting their sex life, the church removed him as a member.[8] Why? Because the Bible is clear: "The wife does not have authority over her own body, but the husband does. Likewise the husband does not have authority over his own body, but the wife does. Do not deprive one another" (1 Cor. 7:4–5). And Proverbs 5 is wisely adding, "Make it fun and frequent!" The word translated "be intoxicated" is used elsewhere in the Old Testament for a man staggering down the street in drunkenness (Isa. 28:7). The point is for a man to be *crazy* in love with his wife. This counsel is not trivial. It is the serious wisdom of God, because, as we shall see later in the Bible, marriage points ultimately to the love of Christ and our joy in him. And the striking thing about this wisdom here in Proverbs, coming from ancient times as it does, is that marriages back then could be arranged for economic or political reasons. But the Bible sweeps all of that aside and calls husbands and wives to be head-over-heels in love with each other.

Second, the other passage in the book of Proverbs comes in

---

8. See Leland Ryken, *Worldly Saints: The Puritans as They Really Were* (Grand Rapids, MI: Zondervan, 1986), 39.

chapter 31. The wise man extols the virtuous wife as a fitting climax to this book of wisdom:

> An excellent wife who can find?
>> She is far more precious than jewels.
> The heart of her husband trusts in her,
>> and he will have no lack of gain. (Prov. 31:10–11)

This woman is a role model. She is a high-capacity woman, very capable as "a helper fit for him." In fact, the phrase "an excellent wife" in verse 10 can be translated more literally "a woman of strength." The Septuagint, the ancient Greek translation of the Hebrew Bible, even renders the phrase as "a manly woman." This iconic woman is *strong*. How so? This poem goes on to say that she works hard, she makes money, she is kind to the poor, she is fearless about the future, she enhances her husband's reputation, she speaks with wisdom, plus more. Verse 17 sums it up: "She dresses herself with strength and makes her arms strong." But she is not using her strengths and abilities to compete with her husband. She is not driven by an identity crisis or treating her marriage as a matter of sexual politics. She is too mature for that. She is giving herself away to her husband, her family, and her community with wholehearted selflessness. A woman of this quality is rare: "An excellent wife who can find? She is far more precious than jewels."

Where the ESV says in verse 11, "[Her husband] will have no lack of gain," the word translated "gain" is "loot, plunder, the spoils of war." Why that wording? Because life is a struggle. This impressive woman is not living in an ideal environment where life comes easily. She is living in the real world. But she is not afraid. She is up to the challenge, and her accomplishments declare her worth. No wonder her husband trusts her. He feels honored to be her husband.

This woman that God gave him is his greatest earthly treasure. In fact, there is only one person this husband trusts more than his wife, and that is God himself. Trust is a very personal and precious gift, especially the trust of the heart. David wrote of the Lord, "In him my heart trusts" (Ps. 28:7). The sage counsels us all, "Trust in the LORD with all your heart" (Prov. 3:5). But here we read, "The heart of her husband trusts in her" (v. 11). That is remarkable. Such a level of intimacy and belonging and connection and dependence and vulnerability can be experienced safely, without betrayal, only in the one-flesh union of marriage. A wife whose proven worth wins and keeps such profound trust is indeed an excellent wife.

The original audience intended for the book of Proverbs was young men, being shaped for leadership in both the royal court and the godly home.[9] Naturally, such men were mostly husbands or husbands-to-be. We men need to know that a wife does not often grow to this level of magnificence on her own. A great wife usually has a great husband. After all, what does the word *husband* mean? We have the related English word *husbandry*, that is, "cultivation." And when the English word *husband* is used as a verb, it means "to cultivate." So here is a husband's privilege and responsibility: to cultivate and nurture his wife. A wise husband's lifetime impact on his wife is that she is enabled to become the magnificent woman, the "excellent wife," God made her to be.

How does a husband do that? Not by browbeating his wife—God doesn't treat us that way—but by encouraging her:

> Her children rise up and call her blessed;
>> her husband also, and he praises her:
> "Many women have done excellently,
>> but you surpass them all."

---

9. See Waltke, *Book of Proverbs: Chapters 1-15*, 58–63.

> Charm is deceitful, and beauty is vain,
>> but a woman who fears the LORD is to be praised.
> Give her of the fruit of her hands,
>> and let her works praise her in the gates.
>>> (Prov. 31:28–31)

Her children rise up, they stand up, and they speak respectfully to their mother. They tell her why they love and admire her. Where did the children learn that? From their father: "He praises her" (v. 28). The key word in these verses is "praise," appearing three times. A wise husband cultivates his wife by setting a high tone of praise and affirmation in their home—not neutral silence, certainly not insults, but bright, positive, life-giving *praise*. The sage is painting a picture of the excellent wife giving herself to her family and to others, and she is receiving praise from her husband and children at home and from her community "in the gates." This biblical vision of a wise marriage displays a husband building his wife up, so that she flourishes in private and in public.[10]

In addition to the book of Proverbs, the wisdom book known as the Song of Solomon takes us discreetly into the bedroom of a godly marriage. We need not be surprised at the lavish eroticism of the Song. Given the marriage theme underlying all of Scripture, how could this book *not* be included? Aspects of the Song's interpretation are much debated.[11] But its overall message is clear as an unblushing celebration of married romance and sexual passion. It is an Old Testament declaration of the New Testament admonition, "Let marriage be held in honor among all, and let the marriage bed

---

10. These expositions of Proverbs 5 and 31 draw from Raymond C. Ortlund Jr., *Proverbs: Wisdom That Works* (Wheaton, IL: Crossway, 2012), 89–96, 149–56.

11. H. H. Rowley, *The Servant of the Lord and Other Essays on the Old Testament* (Oxford, UK: Blackwell, 1965), 197: "There is no book of the Old Testament which has found greater variety of interpretation than the Song of Songs."

be undefiled" (Heb. 13:4). The purpose of the Song is that in marriage, men would be men and women would be women.

The joyously yearning, pursuing tone of the Song of Solomon is far from the clinical detachment of modern sexual research. The Song "is not simply a Kinsey report on the sexual behavior of the ancient male and female. It speaks of other elements in the love relationship that make it full and meaningful."[12] The striking thing about the Song is the pure and gentle loveliness of its eroticism, free from both cold analytics and coarse crudity. It is honest, realistic, hopeful, sincere, playful, tender, awestruck, and reverent throughout. The phrase "as is fitting in the Lord" (Col. 3:18) comes to mind. Biblical love expresses itself fully, in every appropriate way, with sensitive moral aesthetics, because, as the Book of Common Prayer instructs us, marriage is not "to be entered into unadvisedly or lightly, but reverently, discreetly, advisedly, soberly, and in the fear of God." The Song of Solomon strongly agrees.

The Song comes to a focal point with instruction, and even pleading, in chapter 8. The wife pours out her heart to her husband:

> Set me as a seal upon your heart,
>   as a seal upon your arm,
> for love is strong as death,
>   jealousy is fierce as the grave.
> Its flashes are flashes of fire,
>   the very flame of the LORD. (Song 8:6)

To paraphrase and expand what she is saying: "Make me near and dear to you forever. Wear your wedding ring proudly, so that everyone can see your loyalty to me. For this love we share is powerful

---

12. Robert B. Laurin, "The Song of Songs and its Modern Message," *Christianity Today*, August 3, 1962, 11.

in its finality and permanent in its demand, like death itself. In our one-flesh marriage, I am giving myself to you in a way I can never take back. The power of our love burns too intensely to be betrayed without extreme pain, and the Lord himself is the one who made it so. Our love is *sacred*. It must not be violated. It is worthy of our all. Our romance came down from above."

> Many waters cannot quench love,
>> neither can floods drown it.
> If a man offered for love
>> all the wealth of his house,
>> he would be utterly despised. (Song 8:7)

Rather than quenched by the dreary waves of monotonous daily life, real love sweeps us away by its overwhelming power. Falling in love is a kind of temporary insanity, hurling us into the reckless abandon that marital commitment truly is. Fortunately, in a healthy marriage, though we recover our right minds to some degree, the sweet craziness never completely leaves us. As the years roll by, a married couple inevitably suffers the buffetings of this life. But biblical marriage is resilient, for "many waters cannot quench love."

The rugged permanence God intends for married love puts it far beyond the reach of money—and this, said by the vastly wealthy Solomon (1 Kings 10:23). Real love is not for sale. It is so precious that it can only be given away freely. Compared with love, money is contemptible. Anyone oblivious to that would be "utterly despised." But married love is to be joyously revered "as long as you both shall live."

The inviolable sanctity setting married love apart hints at a love yet more sacred. All of us who are married fall short of the high standard of true marital love. Solomon certainly did. And the title of this book in our English Bible is the "Song of Solomon," which is valid. But in the Hebrew Bible the title is the "Song of Songs." This "X of Xs" form of expression registers the superlative degree, like "the Holy of Holies" as the holiest place or "the King of kings" as the highest king. Even so, "The Song of Songs" is Solomon's best song, his number-one hit. We know from 1 Kings 4:29–34 that Solomon, like a Renaissance man of many abilities, wrote 1,005 songs. Jonathan Edwards comments about this best of Solomon's many songs:

> This one song of his which is inserted in the canon of the Scripture is distinguished from all the rest by the name of the Song of Songs, or the most excellent of his songs, or more than all his other songs, as the subject of it is transcendency of a more sublime and excellent nature than the rest, treating of the divine love, union, and communion of the most glorious lovers, Christ and his spiritual spouse, of which a marriage union and conjugal love (which, perhaps, many of the rest of his songs treated of) is but a shadow.[13]

Married love is nothing less than "the very flame of the LORD." But still more sacred is "love divine, all loves excelling," as the old hymn says. If the Song of Solomon is his best song because its vision suggests the love that excels even the best human marriage, then we may read the rest of the Bible as an unfolding symphony of the divine romance, which "many waters cannot quench."

The Prophets

A theme that emerges gradually but strikingly and even daringly, as the Old Testament concludes its love story, is the ultimate

---

13. Jonathan Edwards, *The Works of Jonathan Edwards: Sermons and Discourses, 1720–1723,* ed. Wilson H. Kimnach (New Haven, CT: Yale University Press, 1992), 155.

marriage—the union of the Lord with his people Israel. This thread is woven into the literary fabric early on, with a few denunciations of spiritually lewd behavior as "whoredom" against the Lord, in the law and historical books.[14] But it is the prophets who raise their voices loudly, repeatedly, and disturbingly against the violated marriage of the Lord with his people, using the distasteful language of "whore" and "whoredom" over sixty times. And these references are not sporadic or marginal but are developed into sustained narratives, as in Ezekiel 16 and 23 and Hosea 1–3. In this surprising way the prophets explain Israel's favored status with the Lord, their own shocking betrayals of him, and his final judgment of them in Israel's national decline and eventual collapse. The bride of God sinking to the level of a whore, destroying the most sacred marriage of all, is a major theme in the Prophets.[15]

The primary voices are Isaiah, Jeremiah, Ezekiel, and Hosea, who retell the whole of Israel's history in a new way—as a tragic romance. The Lord gave himself to Israel in a pure and holy marriage. He pledged himself to her to be her God, for all that that means, and she consented to be his, for all that that means. He promised to guide her infallibly, protect her fiercely, fulfill her satisfyingly. She promised to love him, obey him, honor him. But this most sacred marriage failed most miserably. Though the divine husband was faithful, true, and generous, the bride sold out. She gave herself away to many lovers many times. And she was not shy about it. She hurled herself with abandon into her pattern of open and even compulsive whoredom.

But what were the literal realities to which these prophets were pointing by the whoredom metaphor? Because of the comprehensive

---

14. See Ex. 34:16; Lev. 17:7; 20:5–6; Num. 15:39; Deut. 31:16; Judg. 2:17; 8:27, 33; 2 Kings 9:22; 1 Chron. 5:25; 2 Chron. 21:11, 13.

15. See Raymond C. Ortlund Jr., *God's Unfaithful Wife: A Biblical Theology of Spiritual Adultery* (Downers Grove, IL: InterVarsity Press, 1996), 47–136.

"one flesh" nature of marriage, the prophets rightly saw whoredom in every departure from the Lord. The problem with Israel was her compartmentalized religion. She was oblivious to the actual moral nature of her many compromises, "desensitized to desecration,"[16] as long as she kept up the outward rites of Israelite religion. But, specifically, the prophets denounced as a violation of Israel's marriage to God her social injustice, lamented by Isaiah:

> How the faithful city
>> has become a whore,
>> she who was full of justice!
> Righteousness lodged in her,
>> but now murderers. (Isa. 1:21)

Another violation was Israel's idolatrous worship of other gods, which Jeremiah describes with mixed metaphors, taking the whoredom theme beyond the human to an animalian extreme:

> For long ago I broke your yoke
>> and burst your bonds;
>> but you said, "I will not serve."
> Yes, on every high hill
>> and under every green tree
>> you bowed down like a whore.
> Yet I planted you a choice vine,
>> wholly of pure seed.
> How then have you turned degenerate
>> and become a wild vine?
> Though you wash yourself with lye
>> and use much soap,

---

16. John White, *The Golden Cow: Materialism in the Twentieth-Century Church* (Downers Grove, IL: InterVarsity Press, 1979), 121–35.

> the stain of your guilt is still before me, declares the
>   Lord God.
> How can you say, "I am not unclean,
>   I have not gone after the Baals"?
> Look at your way in the valley;
>   know what you have done—
> a restless young camel running here and there,
>   a wild donkey used to the wilderness,
> in her heat sniffing the wind!
>   Who can restrain her lust?
> None who seek her need weary themselves;
>   in her month they will find her. (Jer. 2:20–24)

And Ezekiel discerns in Israel's military and commercial entanglements with foreign nations the same impulse of a prostituted sellout:

> You also played the whore with the Egyptians, your lustful neighbors, multiplying your whoring, to provoke me to anger. Behold, therefore, I stretched out my hand against you and diminished your allotted portion and delivered you to the greed of your enemies, the daughters of the Philistines, who were ashamed of your lewd behavior. You played the whore also with the Assyrians, because you were not satisfied; yes, you played the whore with them, and still you were not satisfied. You multiplied your whoring also with the trading land of Chaldea, and even with this you were not satisfied. (Ezek. 16:26–29)

In various ways, the people of God treated their divine husband as if he were unworthy and inadequate, so that they ran off to other lovers to offset the Lord's perceived failures. Ezekiel says that the people of God eventually sank to a level of degeneracy unheard of among ordinary prostitutes, in that the whore Israel actually paid her customers (Ezek. 16:33–34)!

The shocking reality is this: it was the people of God who made the garden of Eden into the brothel of this world. It was the people of God who were filled not with the Holy Spirit but with "a spirit of whoredom" (Hos. 4:12; 5:4), so that nothing was sacred and everything had a price. Eventually, after his promiscuous wife had invited too many other lovers into their bed too many times, and she lay there spent and wasted and exhausted, "worn out by adultery" (Ezek. 23:43), God gave her up.

There is a reason why the last two words of the Prophets are "utter destruction" (Mal. 4:6). The marital union between the Lord and his people became so limited rather than all-encompassing, the relationship was so opposite to "one flesh," the sanctity of their union was so extremely violated, that the judgment of God fell hard. It appeared that the sin of man had defeated the promises of God. Who could dare hold out hope, when Jerusalem lay in smoldering ruins, its walls broken down, its treasures looted, its temple desecrated, its people exiled, its mission defeated, God's presence removed? Obviously, the marriage was over.

But God is able to rekindle a dead romance.

3

Marriage in the New Testament

The biblical definition of marriage established in Genesis 2:24—one mortal life fully shared between one man and one woman—that Old Testament definition is clearly reaffirmed as normative in the New Testament. Three times the New Testament quotes Genesis 2:24 as the unchanging and glorious meaning of marriage today and until the end of time.

The first reaffirmation of Genesis 2:24 comes from Jesus himself, when the Pharisees ask him about divorce. Their interest, as always, is more procedural and technical and hairsplitting. His eyes see through all that into the true glory of marriage:

> And Pharisees came up to him and tested him by asking, "Is it lawful to divorce one's wife for any cause?" He answered, "Have you not read that he who created them from the beginning made them male and female, and said, 'Therefore a man shall leave his father and his mother and hold fast to his wife, and the two shall become one flesh'? So they are no longer two but one flesh. What therefore God has joined

together, let not man separate." They said to him, "Why then did Moses command one to give a certificate of divorce and to send her away?" He said to them, "Because of your hardness of heart Moses allowed you to divorce your wives, but from the beginning it was not so. And I say to you: whoever divorces his wife, except for sexual immorality, and marries another, commits adultery." The disciples said to him, "If such is the case of a man with his wife, it is better not to marry." (Matt. 19:3–10)

It is obvious that Jesus is defining marriage in a way not limited to the garden of Eden but meant for our broken world today, because he is answering a question about divorce. And his teaching so clearly recovers and so strongly reaffirms the original, glorious vision of marriage in Genesis that his disciples are astonished: "If such is the case of a man with his wife, it is better not to marry" (v. 10). Jesus did not lower the standard.

When asked to adjudicate the difficult question of divorce, Jesus went immediately to Genesis 1 and 2 for his wisdom, as if that were the natural and obvious thing to do. In verse 4 he appeals to Genesis 1:27, and in verse 5 he appeals to Genesis 2:24. Clearly, Jesus regarded the Genesis account as authoritative. He did not say about Genesis 2:24, in particular, "Sure, we all know that old verse. But it doesn't apply anymore. We've moved on." Jesus treated Genesis 2:24 as filled with exactly the insight into marriage that we need today as we think through our marital problems. So he not only believed Genesis 2:24 to be valid and relevant, but he publicly taught it to be so—and not because he was a man of his times, echoing what everyone believed back then. What got Jesus into trouble was that he was *not* a man of his times. He thought for himself, he spoke boldly out of his sincere convictions, and he never minded disagreeing strongly with anyone. Yes, Jesus allowed himself to be addressed as Rabbi, the traditional honor given to a teacher (John 1:38). But he did not teach as one more rabbinic voice within the line of Jewish tradition; he taught as the only Son of the Father. With both humility and confidence Jesus claimed, "I do nothing on my own authority, but speak just as the Father taught me" (John 8:28). Unlike every other great teacher, Jesus believed, spoke, and taught not as one who had risen up out of history but as one who had been sent down from above. Moreover, he imparted to all his followers who faithfully receive his message the same sense of being commissioned by an authority altogether unearthly: "As the Father has sent me, even so I am sending you" (John 20:21). Therefore, when Jesus treats Genesis 2:24 as definitional of marriage in the world today, every true follower of Jesus will pay attention.

Jesus advances our understanding of marriage, according to Genesis 2:24, in two ways. First, Jesus read the simple word "they" in "*they* shall become one flesh," and he made its meaning clear beyond all doubt. That true marriage, as originally given in the garden of Eden, involves two people only, one man with one woman, which should have been obvious all along simply from the facts of the matter. But Solomon, a wise man in other respects, found a way around the plain meaning of the Genesis text, for he had seven hundred trophy wives (1 Kings 11:3). Jesus did not approve of polygamy. He approved of the monogamy God had established for all time in Eden. So our Lord made the obvious still more obvious, leaving no "wiggle room" at all, when he said, "*The two* shall become one flesh" (v. 5).[1] We therefore assert again that the biblical story is not

---

1. The wording of the Matthew text is not exactly identical with the Septuagint rendering of Gen. 2:24, according to the Göttingen edition. But the key words, "the two," do appear in the LXX tradition. Whether or not Jesus was speaking from within that textual tradition is immaterial to my point. He validated the truth it communicates.

crowded with multiple and equally legitimate models of marriage, so that its standard is unclear. Jesus himself settled the question. He meant to.

This is a good place to add an aside about how to read the Bible. We see here in Jesus our best guide to biblical interpretation. The way he reads the Bible is grounded in a certain preunderstanding he brings to the Bible. He hints at it in verse 4, "from the beginning," and again in verse 8, "but from the beginning it was not so." Jesus shows that how the Bible begins must take precedence. This leads us to realize that the structure of the Bible as a whole shapes how we interpret its parts. The Bible starts with a glorious beginning (Genesis 1–2), then moves quickly to a catastrophic betrayal and precipitous decline (Genesis 3–11), and then to a growing body of divine promises of grace intermixed with many episodes of human failure (Genesis 12–Malachi 4), leading to Jesus in his life, death, burial, resurrection, and ascension, the spread of the gospel out into the nations, his second coming, the final judgment, and the greater glory of his renewed creation (Matthew 1–Revelation 22). So the Bible is not flat literary terrain. The Bible is built as a growing narrative, with a trajectory of progressive revelation trending toward the renewal of all things. And the point is this: all the parts of the Bible along the way cannot be rightly understood if they are detached from the grand narrative starting in the creation and culminating in Jesus. And it is the end that finally explains the beginning and the middle. The Pharisees did not think like Jesus. They were looking narrowly at this divorce law by itself. They were drilling down into the mind of Moses, as if that were enough. Jesus connected this law with the larger biblical narrative. So he was able to see it more profoundly.

The Quran is not structured like the Bible. The Sura "Women," the fourth of 114 Suras, tells a Muslim man, "Marry such women as seem good to you, two, three, four," and, "And those [wives] you fear may be rebellious admonish; banish them to their couches, and beat them."[2] But the Quran does not take those instructions into greater light the way the Bible advances beyond the law of Moses. The structure of the Quran is such that having ruled in favor of polygamy and wife beating, there it stands, unresolved.

Jesus reads the Old Testament in such a way as to restore a message lost from the glorious beginning, something obscured during the long period of decline. He is reestablishing the norm God intended from the beginning and preparing the way for further revelation, as we shall see later in this chapter. The rest of the New Testament follows his way of thinking, because Jesus taught his apostles how to interpret the Old Testament (Luke 24:44–45; Acts 1:3). So the question astute readers of the Bible will always be asking is, Where is the Bible taking this theme or doctrine or command or insight, especially in light of Jesus, the key to it all? No biblical statement is a flat assertion standing in isolation, interpretable by itself alone. End of aside.

The Lord's second insight goes deeper than the obvious. Indeed, it is amazing. Jesus read the perhaps ambiguous word "become" in "they shall *become* one flesh," and he saw something there that we might never have thought of. Behind the word "become" Jesus sees a personal power at work. He sees no one less than God: "What therefore *God* has joined together . . ." (v. 6). A husband and wife, when they marry, do not become one flesh by their own wills or by the pastor's pronouncement or by some mysterious process. *God* joins them together (Mal. 2:14–15).

This is why, as a pastor, when I provide premarital counseling for an engaged couple, I always try to tell them something like this:

---

2. Arthur J. Arberry, *The Koran Interpreted* (Oxford, UK: Oxford University Press, 1964), 72, 77–78.

"On your wedding day, you will not be there to entertain an audience. You can ignore the crazy hoopla of the typical American wedding today. I hope you will relax and enjoy this wonderful moment, because there will be only three important people there at your wedding ceremony: the bride, the groom, and God. The rest of us will be, properly speaking, mere witnesses to what God will be accomplishing between the two of you. *He* will be present, joining you together, soldering you together, uniting you together as 'one flesh' for the rest of your earthly days."

What Jesus says here is so striking and so sacred that it deserves to become a conviction we all revere and remain loyal to, as the definition of marriage is being expanded today and even blurred into just another convenient social arrangement of our own devising. Here is the conviction our Lord is imparting to us. It is true not only that God was present when he joined Adam and Eve together as one flesh. It is true not only that God is present in the institution of marriage in general. But it is also true that God is present in every lawful marriage in particular. Jesus is talking here about marriages that fail, marriages that end up in divorce. And he is pushing back against the cheapening of marriage by showing us how grand every lawful marriage really is: "What therefore *God* has joined together, let not man separate" (v. 6).

If you are married, even if your marriage in some ways disappoints you, still, God was the one who joined you two together. Your imperfect marriage in the world of today is as sacred in the sight of God as was the perfect marriage between Adam and Eve in the garden of Eden. Your marriage is a grace from above. Your marriage is a miracle. Your marriage came to you with the touch of God upon it, and it remains dear to him. Your marriage has the potential, by his grace, to bring redemption into the broken world we all live in now. Your imperfect marriage is, therefore, worth celebrating. Jesus thought so.

The second reaffirmation of Genesis 2:24 in the New Testament comes from the apostle Paul. The morally casual lifestyles of the Christians in Corinth were trivializing their bodies as of no gospel significance. Every right-thinking Christian will know that the body is not the crowning human experience (Rom. 8:5–8). But neither is the body nothing. It is far from nothing. In this passage Paul teaches us a theology of the human body as something glorious. For the Christian, his or her body has been made a sacred location of God's redemptive presence in the world:

> Do you not know that your bodies are members of Christ? Shall I then take the members of Christ and make them members of a prostitute? Never! Or do you not know that he who is joined to a prostitute becomes one body with her? For, as it is written, "The two will become one flesh." But he who is joined to the Lord becomes one spirit with him. Flee from sexual immorality. Every other sin a person commits is outside the body, but the sexually immoral person sins against his own body. Or do you not know that your body is a temple of the Holy Spirit within you, whom you have from God? You are not your own, for you were bought with a price. So glorify God in your body. (1 Cor. 6:15–20)

If the Bible did not say this clearly, would we dare to believe it? Would it even have occurred to us as a possibility? But Paul treats it as something so obvious that all Christians should be aware of this: "Do you not know that your bodies are members of Christ?" (v. 15). Amazingly, the gospel reveals that our bodies, the humblest part of us, are members of Christ, limbs of Christ, organs of Christ.

Epictetus, a younger contemporary of Paul and an influential Stoic philosopher, taught this:

> Inasmuch as these two elements were comingled in our begetting, on the one hand the body, which we have in common with the brutes, and, on the other, reason and intelligence, which we have in common with the gods, some of us incline toward the former relationship, which is unblessed by fortune and is mortal, and only a few toward that which is divine and blessed.[3]

If I did not believe the gospel, Epictetus's view would seem to me plausible. I could understand myself his way. I have my spiritual and intellectual self, which is more heavenly and godlike, but I tend to neglect it. And I have my physical and visceral self, which is more earthly and animal-like, and its impulses and appetites I tend to obey. And my salvation would lie in my spiritual self subduing and dominating my physical self. But this is not the Christian gospel, for the Word became flesh (John 1:14).

The gospel claims that our bodies—not just our souls, but our bodies, with all their appetites and drives, with all their smells and messes, with all their aches and pains, with all their sneezing and yawning—yes, our *bodies* are united to the living Christ. We are physical extensions of Christ in the modern world. So, for example, our legs are how Jesus walks the streets of our cities today. He so cares for us in all that we are, he so identifies with us, he so gets involved with us, that every part of our very bodies, *including our sexuality*, is eternally joined to him now and brings his incarnational presence into the world we live in. Could our bodies have

---

3. Epictetus, *Epictetus: The Discourses as Reported by Arrian, Books I–II*, trans. W. A. Oldfather, Loeb Classical Library (Cambridge, MA: Harvard University Press, 2000), 25.

any greater dignity? Can we now allow ourselves to trivialize our sexual behavior as of little consequence, as long as our hearts glow with love for the Lord? The Christian gospel creates strong sexual integrity not by despising the body but by honoring the body.

Here is the apostle's point in the rest of verse 15. I will summarize it by expanding and paraphrasing the sense: "Shall I then take the sexuality of Christ and join his sexuality to a prostitute? Shall I take the eyes of Christ and the brain of Christ and make them members of porn? Shall I take any member of my body, which Christ now claims as dear and precious to himself, as if my body were his very own body, because it is, and use my/his body for any sinful purpose at all? *Never!*"

If our poor bodies could somehow speak for themselves, they would plead with us, "Oh, please, don't take me there! Please don't do that with me! I belong to Jesus now. He cares about me, even if you don't. He values me, even if you would abuse me. Oh, have mercy upon me and don't do such horrible things with me! In fact, don't even think of me. Think of Jesus, and treat me as a part of him, because I am!" Here then is how our standards of sexual behavior are elevated and preserved—the love of Jesus reaching out and embracing us, all that we are, as genuine members of his holiness.

In verse 16 Paul quotes part of Genesis 2:24 with yet another insight: "Or do you not know that he who is joined to a prostitute becomes one body with her? For, as it is written, 'The two will become one flesh.'" Paul is saying that sexual sin mimics one-flesh marriage with a mere one-body coupling. He makes that point by quoting Genesis 2:24 as the standard of true marriage and true sexual union. So Genesis 2:24 not only honors married sex, but it also condemns unmarried sex. Now we see that the biblical vision of marriage not only includes what is right, but it also excludes what is wrong. The relevance of Genesis 2:24 extends beyond marriage itself; it addresses, by implication, the entire range of questions about manhood and womanhood and human sexuality.

But Paul must put into place another piece of the puzzle, in verse 17, for us to grasp the full significance of Genesis 2:24 and the biblical definition of marriage: "But he who is joined to the Lord becomes one spirit with him." Paul lays alongside the phrase "joined to a prostitute" in verse 16 the new phrase "joined to the Lord" in verse 17. He uses the same language in both, because spiritual union is analogous to sexual union. These two unions, sexual and spiritual, are comparable—though incompatible, the way that the Corinthians were living them out.

What we are now able to understand, from verses 16 and 17, is three categories of personal union. "One body" is sexual sin. "One flesh" is human marriage. "One spirit" is *the* marriage. And here is how these three categories of personal union relate to the ultimate reality, who is Christ. "One body" is incompatible with *the* marriage, "one flesh" is compatible with *the* marriage, and "one spirit" is the beginning of *the* marriage. So the larger, weightier point that Paul is establishing is this: sexual sin does more than complicate a human marriage, though it certainly does that. But even more, sexual sin violates *the* marriage. If you love Jesus, you are joined to the Lord as "one spirit" with him, which is the most profound kind of personal union. You are loved. You are claimed. You belong to another above. You are married at the deepest level of your being.[4] Whatever losses and sufferings you might endure in this life, you are in the marital embrace of the Son of God now and forever.[5]

---

4. In 2 Cor. 11:1–3 Paul says that we are engaged to Christ, while here in 1 Corinthians 6 he says that we are already joined to Christ in a marital way. But we are both engaged, in one sense, and also married, in another sense. We are engaged, in that the great consummation awaits our arrival in heaven (Rev. 19:7, 9). But we are also married, in that we now belong fully to him. Our arrival in heaven will change our condition but not our status.

5. The ultimate marriage is so meaningful to Paul that, as he will explain in the next chapter of this letter, single believers in this present age even have an advantage over married believers.

Therefore, the command of verse 18 becomes intensely meaningful: "Flee from sexual immorality. Every other sin a person commits is outside the body, but the sexually immoral person sins against his own body." As Anselm put it long ago, "If we must fight against other sins, we must flee from fornication."[6] Joseph stands out as an example of this practical wisdom (Gen. 39:11–12). It is foolish to see how close we can get to sexual sin before we actually cross the line. God calls us to *run*.

Why the urgency? Because sexual sin involves such physical intimacy that we desecrate the temple of the Lord that our physicality has now become. Other sins do not violate the "one spirit" union the way "one body" does, because the Spirit of the Lord is present within our bodies. Making the sexual members of Christ into the members of a prostitute makes the sacred temple of the Holy Spirit into a whorehouse. The thought might be shocking initially. But if we stop and think about it, do we not know this? "Do you not know that your body is a temple of the Holy Spirit within you?" (v. 19). To defile the temple of God is an *extreme* sin. But we have been claimed by an *extreme* grace: "You are not your own, for you were bought with a price. So glorify God in your body" (vv. 19b–20).

The gospel argument for all sexual integrity, both for married people and unmarried people, draws from the entire sweep of the biblical drama of redemption, from Genesis 2:24 and the garden of Eden, through the moral sewers of this present evil age where God comes down to make our bodies into sacred temples, on to the glorious resurrection at the end of time: "God . . . will also raise us up by his power" (1 Cor. 6:14). There is nothing legalistic and petty

---

The unmarried believer is more absorbed with the things of the Lord and how to please him and bear fruit for him, while the attention of the married believer must of necessity be to some extent divided (1 Cor. 7:32–38).

6. Quoted in F. Godet, *Commentary on St. Paul's First Epistle to the Corinthians* (Edinburgh: T&T Clark, 1889), 1:311.

and narrow about biblical sexual ethics. And what helps us right now, in our moments of weakness and temptation, is the amazing reality that we are now filled with the glory of God, not just in our personalities but in our very bodies too. God has made each of us into a sacred temple, where Jesus is to be worshiped and served. And it cost him to remake us in this wonderful way. He paid a price—his very lifeblood on the cross. Therefore, we are no longer our own. We belong to him now.

Here is another way to think about it. I try to drive carefully. But when I happen to borrow a friend's car, I drive *very* carefully. I don't want to damage the property of a friend and return it to him all banged up. Even so, our bodies are the personal property of someone else. The only way we could say, "Who does he think he is, telling me what to do with my body?"—the only way we could say that is by *not* belonging to him at all. Did he shed his blood to cover our sins? Has he given his Spirit to make us new? If so, then we should glorify him even in our physicality, especially our sexuality.

One final word on this passage. Notice what the apostle Paul is not saying here. He is not saying, "If you will glorify God in your body, then he will wash your sins away in the blood of Jesus, he will indwell you by his Spirit, and he will raise you bodily on the final day." That would be law. But this is gospel. What is the Word of God saying to us here? "In the past I covered your sins with the blood of Jesus, in the present my Spirit indwells you, and in the future I will raise you bodily into total glory. Therefore, glorify me in your body right now, moment by moment."

The third time the New Testament reaffirms Genesis 2:24 is again by the apostle Paul when he coaches the Ephesian Christians in how to build gospel-centered marriages. The amazing thing about this quotation of Genesis 2:24 is that the apostle uses it to point beyond human marriage to the ultimate marriage. The biblical love story is now moving toward its glorious conclusion. But before all of God's people arrive there, married Christians in the present time can display something of the ultimate marriage through their own marriages. Here is how, first addressing Christian wives:

> Wives, submit to your own husbands, as to the Lord. For the husband is the head of the wife even as Christ is the head of the church, his body, and is himself its Savior. Now as the church submits to Christ, so also wives should submit in everything to their husbands. (Eph. 5:22–24)

The first verse of the chapter blankets everything that follows in this way: "Be imitators of God, as beloved children" (Eph. 5:1). There is nothing about the gospel that is degrading or unworthy. It lifts us up, giving us free access into the practical wisdom of God our loving Father. So what does that look like for a Christian wife?

Paul's counsel draws upon the head-with-helper relational paradigm of Genesis 2. He does not set this marital model aside or even modify it, but he fills it out further, and in a striking way. The call to a wife—submit to your own husband—Paul links not with the order of creation but, even more grandly, with the entire drama of redemption in Christ.[7] That is why Paul does not apologize for a wife's submission to her husband, as if it were a merely human cultural construct. The apostle was aware of human cultures.[8] He was quite prepared to critique a human culture: "One of the Cretans, a prophet of their own, said, 'Cretans are always liars, evil beasts, lazy gluttons.' This testimony is true. Therefore rebuke them sharply"

---

7. Paul sees and respects the order of creation, and elsewhere he does use it to validate his teaching (1 Cor. 11:7–9; 1 Tim. 2:12–13).

8. See, e.g., 1 Cor. 9:20–21; 10:32; Gal. 2:7–9, 11–14; 3:28; Eph. 2:11–22; Col. 3:11.

(Titus 1:12–13). But here Paul dignifies a pattern of marital submission as the primary way a Christian wife exemplifies the gospel.[9]

Still, a wife's submission to her husband is difficult for many to accept today. It can seem archaic. And our trust has been betrayed at times. So let's press further into the apostle's teaching with three questions.

First, what does it mean to submit? First and foremost, a mentality of submission is to sweeten the entire Christian community. Immediately preceding this word to Christian wives, Paul urges us all, "... *submitting* to one another out of reverence for Christ" (v. 21). The glorious presence of Christ among us flavors all true Christian relationships with a voluntary spirit of servanthood. The example of Jesus sets a tone of humility among us as well: "In *humility* count others more significant than yourselves" (Phil. 2:3). The gospel of freedom never creates an ethos of swagger and self-assertion but the opposite: "Through love *serve* one another" (Gal. 5:13). That word translated "serve" is a strong one. It is also used for the service of a slave (1 Tim. 6:2). Jesus, when he humbly picked up the towel and the basin of a slave and washed his disciples' feet, said, "I have given you an example, that you also should do just as I have done to you" (John 13:15). It is clear, then, that the constant attitude within a faithful Christian community is a Christlike readiness to submit, that is, to adjust and adapt, to fit in, to help make it work, to find the win/win outcome, and at a personal price too.

For a wife in particular, God calls her to live out this Christian mentality of submission toward her husband, as toward no other. Her submission is not a servile groveling, because she submits to her husband "as the church submits to Christ" (v. 24), which is dignifying to us all. Her submission is of the same high quality as the

---

9. Submission to her husband is the entirety of Paul's instruction to a Christian wife in Col. 3:18. It is the primary message of the apostle Peter to a Christian wife in 1 Pet. 3:1–6.

spirit of every faithful Christian. But what is unique to a Christian wife is her voluntary deference to her husband, "for the husband is the head of the wife even as Christ is the head of the church" (v. 23). The New Testament never tells a husband to subjugate his wife. An imperious husband knows nothing of the mind of Christ. Instead, the New Testament calls a Christian husband to enter into his wife's hardships with sympathetic understanding, because she is his equal, a helper fit for him and a fellow heir of the grace of life (1 Pet. 3:7). But the calling of the wife, for her part, is an attitude of readiness to yield to and support her husband's worthy headship.

The opposite of a submissive spirit is an unsatisfiable demand-ingness, a fault-finding resistance, a tiresome fretfulness: "A continual dripping on a rainy day and a quarrelsome wife are alike" (Prov. 27:15). No man gets married in order to live under the leaky roof, so to speak, of a nagging, scolding wife. Life at home should never be made into a dripping water torture. A man's home, the place of refuge, must not be yet more of the storm he must cope with every day at work. But a wise Christian wife, with "a gentle and quiet spirit" (1 Pet. 3:4), refreshes her husband's spirit to face the challenge of life again the next day with new determination and confidence.

This delicate relational pattern of head with helper, the head taking responsibility and providing initiative, the helper supporting, encouraging, comforting—this is too beautiful to be regimented. There is no one-size-fits-all way to follow through. But a wife's submissive heart toward her faithful husband is a pattern, a design, clearly taught in the New Testament. It is filled with potential for displaying the gospel before family, friends, neighbors, and colleagues, some of whom might never come into a church to hear the gospel. What's more, the New Testament offers no alternative design, no pattern of marital life that excludes the submission of a wife. Naturally and rightly, a wife will at times disagree with her husband. She will think for herself. She will ask questions, express her reservations, and help her husband see a problem from another angle of vision. Her counsel will add value to her husband. And a wise husband will seek his wife's input. Still, in the end, the husband is uniquely responsible to bear the burden as head. And a Christian wife will always want to be asking herself, "How can I represent to my husband something of the church's joyful submission to Christ our head?"

Many practical questions could be asked at this point. Other appropriate qualifications could be added. But this is not the kind of book for exploring those possibilities. If suffices here to say that a wife's heart, welcoming her husband's headship, is not reducible to a set of legalistic rules. Christian marriage is like a waltz, not a military march. By trusting the Lord and embracing her calling, a Christian wife empowers her husband as no one else on the face of the earth can do. She is so secure in Christ that she is no longer jealous to establish her identity separate from her husband. She understands how profound it is to be one flesh with him, and she gives him her whole heart and her practical support.

Second, why does Paul add the words "as to the Lord" in verse 22? "Wives, submit to your own husbands, *as to the Lord.*" Is Paul leaving room for a husband to play God? No. He is saying that a Christian wife's submission is, in the final analysis, not really to her husband but to the Lord. Her gracious disposition to receive and affirm her husband's headship is nothing less than a sacred act of worship to God, and he receives it and prizes it highly. The Bible says that a wife's gentle and quiet spirit "in God's sight is very precious" (1 Pet. 3:4). When a husband does not appreciate how sweetly his wife keeps looking for ways to make things work, God does see, and he does appreciate her. She is always very precious to him.

Third, what about the words in verse 24: "in everything"? Paul says, "So also wives should submit *in everything* to their husbands." Does that mean a husband has the right to ask his wife to do whatever he asks, even to sin? No. It means that there is no area of her life that she cordons off from her husband. There is no part of her life that she keeps to herself only and says to her husband, "You have no place here. You keep out." To be one flesh in marriage is all-encompassing, like no other relationship. Even the best friendship stops short of "in everything." But a wife's submission to her husband, as to the Lord, in everything is a powerful display of the gospel in human form. In a wife like this, people can see how the gospel works at a practical level. It might make an eternal difference for them.

Paul instructs husbands now, imparting such a vision of Christlike loving care that it might take our breath away. Far from suppressing his wife or even just putting up with her, a Christian husband should actively love her toward *magnificence*, the way Christ loves his church, "so that he might present the church to himself in splendor" (v. 27). That word *splendor* reminds us of the New Testament doctrine of glorification, which says that God's purpose toward us is not merely to make us nice people but to make us *glorious* people with something of his own glory (2 Thess. 2:14). This word *splendor* suggests that glory, an uncommon and highly esteemed status of honor. Even so, the gospel fills a husband's heart with a sense of his wife's greatness and potential, the glorious woman she is destined to become, and he learns to love her accordingly:

> Husbands, love your wives, as Christ loved the church and gave himself up for her, that he might sanctify her, having cleansed her by the washing of water with the word, so that

he might present the church to himself in splendor, without spot or wrinkle or any such thing, that she might be holy and without blemish. In the same way husbands should love their wives as their own bodies. He who loves his wife loves himself. For no one ever hated his own flesh, but nourishes and cherishes it, just as Christ does the church, because we are members of his body. "Therefore a man shall leave his father and mother and hold fast to his wife, and the two shall become one flesh." This mystery is profound, and I am saying that it refers to Christ and the church. (Eph. 5:25–32)

There is no higher calling for a Christian husband. To be a true head is to love as Christ loved—sacrificially. To be married to a selfish man who, in effect, creates one *more* child in the house—for any wife, that is hard to bear. But a Christlike husband makes her burden lighter. He enjoys serving her as her lover and her provider and her defender, like Christ with his church. But even more deeply, beneath the Christlike behavior, biblical headship flows out of the mind of Christ. Our Savior's own mentality becomes visible in a Christian husband cheerfully taking responsibility to lead, provide for, and protect his wife.[10]

The heart of a Christian husband comes to a focal point in one word, the key word for the husband, in verse 25: "Husbands, *love* your wives, as Christ loved the church and gave himself up for her." The word *love* is wonderful. We can see its sacrificial boldness in this very verse. But this word *love* is overused in our world today. So can we drill down more deeply into this word? Paul helps us to do so, in verse 29. In the coherence of the passage, the words "nourishes" and "cherishes" in verse 29 restate and clarify the meaning of the

---

10. John Piper and Wayne Grudem, eds., *Recovering Biblical Manhood and Womanhood* (Wheaton, IL: Crossway, 1991), 35–45.

word "love": "For no one ever hated his own flesh, but *nourishes* and *cherishes* it, just as Christ does the church." So Christ nourishing and cherishing the church as his own body is equivalent to Christ not hating but loving his church. Christ does not tyrannize us, and neither will a Christian husband lord it over his wife as her head, but quite the opposite. He will nourish and cherish her.

How then do "nourish" and "cherish" help us understand the true meaning of *love*? These words certainly take a husband beyond just bringing home a paycheck. They are words of wholehearted involvement.

The word *nourish* means "to develop, to nurture, to lift up." Paul uses this word in another relational context, in Ephesians 6:4, where he instructs Christian fathers, "Do not provoke your children to anger, but *bring them up* in the discipline and instruction of the Lord." So this word *nourish* is freighted with a sense of dignifying purpose and care and attention.

Therefore, a loving Christian husband cares so deeply about his wife that he makes sure that her life is moving in a desirable direction, even as Christ nourishes us all. Marriage to a Christlike husband is, for a woman, the opposite of a dead-end life. A woman married to a nourishing man comes to the end of her days as an older lady, and as she is sitting on a porch somewhere in her rocking chair looking back on her life, she is praising God and thinking, "Being married to my husband opened my whole life up. Yes, we suffered. Yes, we made mistakes. But in it all, my husband thought of *me*. He cared about how *my* life was going. What a great run we had, living together for Christ!" That is *nourishing* one's wife.

The word *cherish* goes even deeper emotionally, because this word means "to comfort, to warm, to soften" (as by heat). Our word *heartwarming* conveys the sense. Paul uses this word in

1 Thessalonians 2:7, where he says, "We were gentle among you, like a nursing mother *taking care of* her own children."

So when a woman is married to a lovingly Christlike man who cherishes her, she feels warmth in her heart at being valued by her husband and held dear above all others, second only to Christ himself. Her husband doesn't compare her with others or find fault with her or treat her as a loser he is stuck with. That would break her heart. Instead, her husband delights in her and prizes her, and she feels it deep inside with a heartwarming glow. That is *cherishing* one's wife.

We are now ready to appreciate verse 29 as a whole: "For no one ever hated his own flesh, but nourishes and cherishes it, just as Christ does the church." No normal man hates his own body. He might look in the mirror and wish he had a better body in some ways. But he does not savage his body. Instead, a man makes the best of it that he can. Even so, a man's wife will not be ideal in every way. But she is still his wife, one flesh with him, wonderfully bound to him as a dear part of his very self. How could he neglect or despise her, even in her imperfections? No, he will care for her all the more, nourishing and cherishing her toward her destined glory. After all, every one of us gives the Lord plenty of reasons to give up and walk away. But his heart finds in our very offenses only more reasons to stay tenderly involved with us, all the way to our eternal magnificence. *And that is what it means to love.*

But where Paul takes our thinking next is astonishing. Quoting Genesis 2:24, he gives us a surprising insight into marriage, in verses 30–32:

> We are members of his body. "Therefore a man shall leave his father and mother and hold fast to his wife, and the two shall become one flesh." This mystery is profound, and I am saying that it refers to Christ and the church.

Marriage is common. It does not appear profound. In meeting someone new and introducing my wife, Jani, no one has ever said to me, "You're *married*? No way. I mean, I've heard of marriage, but I've never actually met a married couple. This is incredible. Hey everybody, look at this—a married couple!" Marriage does not astound us. That is why Paul alerts us to the "profound mystery" revealed in a Christian marriage. We need new eyes to discern the glory God has put there. There is a reason why marriage appears in Genesis 2. The context is the creation of the universe, in Genesis 1. I have never seen a creation of a universe. But I have seen many weddings. Marriage may be common to us, but it is why the universe was created, and not for Adam and Eve only, but even more for Christ and his church.

Consider how Paul's logic unfolds in these crucial verses. We are members of Christ's body (v. 30). That is, we are very near and dear to him. Paul even stops referring to "the church" and now makes it personal: "*We* are members of his body." It certainly is personal to Christ. By the grace of his cross he so removed every barrier, he so drew us in, he so nourishes and cherishes us now that we occupy a place within his deepest heart. John Calvin writes that as we read these verses in the Bible, "we hear our Lord Jesus Christ call us to himself and tell us that we are so joined to him that he does not have anything of his own which he does not share with us and of which he will not have us as partakers."[11] Christ could not love us more tenderly or identify with us more personally. All of his grace toward us pulses in these words, "We are members of his body." But notice what Paul does with that insight. In verse 31 he explains that *that* is why people get married. The love of Jesus for us is the reason why people get married! Look at the logic: "We are members of his body. '*Therefore*

---

11. John Calvin, *Sermons on The Epistle to the Ephesians* (Edinburgh: Banner of Truth, 1975), 616.

a man shall leave his father and his mother.'" The function of Genesis 2:24 changes in this new context. In Genesis 2, the "Therefore" points back to the fact that Eve was the bone and flesh of Adam. But here in Ephesians 5, the "Therefore" points back to the fact that we are members of Christ's body. So then, why do people feel the stirrings of romance and start spending time together and take long walks hand in hand and long for one another when apart and write poetry and sing along to "our song" and fall so head over heels in love that they finally jump into the mega-commitment of marriage? There is a reason for this very human experience. And the reason is not only what God did back in the garden of Eden with Adam and Eve but also, and even more, what God has done in uniting Christ with his church. The eternal romance—not, in the final analysis, the love of the couple getting married but the love of Jesus for us and our joyful deference to him—the eternal love story is why God created the universe and why God gave us marriage in Eden and why couples fall in love and get married in the world today. Every time a bride and groom stand there and take their vows, they are reenacting the biblical love story, whether they realize it or not. The Son of God stepping down out of eternity, entering time, taking on flesh, pursuing and winning his bride as his very heart and body with his inmost, sincerest love so that he can fit her to be with him forever above—*that dramatic super-reality is the breathtaking reason why human marriage exists.* It is truly profound. And Christian married couples have the privilege of making the mystery of the gospel visible in the world today by living out the dynamic interplay of an Ephesians 5–quality marriage.

We should not think that Christ and the church are the metaphor in this passage, but the reverse. Christ and the church are the reality of realities, and our Christian marriages are the metaphors. The Book of Common Prayer has long taught us that marriage is "an honorable estate, instituted of God, *signifying unto us the mystical union that is betwixt Christ and his Church.*" May every Christian married couple, head with helper, represent and embody and exemplify and incarnate the true romance before all around with their own stunning beauty together. This too is one way we bear the image of God into the world today. And we need not feel an improper pressure about this, as if our marriages must be perfect. The whole point is that no Christian marriage can be the ultimate human experience. But every faithful Christian marriage points beyond itself to the perfect union we all share with the Lord Jesus Christ. Our little metaphorical marriages can always draw strength from the real marriage we share with our Savior.

> However, let each one of you love his wife as himself, and let the wife see that she respects her husband. (Eph. 5:33)

For Paul, the practical demonstration of the gospel in our marriages comes down to love and respect. Every Christian husband who grasps the gospel will love his wife as himself. And every Christian wife who grasps the gospel will respect her husband as her head. His love for her, with her respect for him, will display the eternal romance of Christ and the church, bringing the only lasting hope that exists into a brokenhearted world.

Paul's words about a husband's love and a wife's respect not only lift our eyes to the Christ-with-the-church reality but also prompt us to look back to Adam and Eve in Genesis 2. There is an insight embedded here in the biblical call to love and respect that can help every married couple.

For the husband, remember that God made Eve from Adam, for Adam, as his dear partner in life to help him follow the divine call. But now, in our broken world of today, deep in the heart of every wife is the self-doubt that wonders, "Do I please him? Am I the one he dreamed of and longed for? Will he love me to the end? Am I safe with this man I married? Will he cast me off? Even if we go the distance, will he get tired of me?" A wise husband will understand that that uncertainty, that question, is way down deep in his wife's heart. And he will spend his life speaking into it, gently and tenderly communicating to her in many ways, "Darling, you are the one I want. I cherish you. I rejoice over you, as no other. The thought of living without you is horrible to me. I love the thought of growing old together with you, hand in hand all the way. I will hold you close to my heart until my dying day." A wise husband prizes and praises his wife above all others. That is why the word *love* is in verse 33. Love breathes life into a woman.

For the wife, remember that God made Adam first and put him in the garden with a job to do, a mission to fulfill, a mountain to climb. But now, in our broken world of today, deep in the heart of every man is the self-doubt that wonders, "Am I man enough to meet the challenge God has called me to? Can I fulfill my destiny? Won't I end up failing? Is there any point in even trying?" That question is way down deep inside the heart of every husband. A wise wife will understand that. And she will spend her life speaking into it, communicating to her husband in many ways, "Honey, I believe in you. I know you can follow God's call, by God's grace, for God's glory. The Lord is with you, and so am I. Let's go for it!" A wise wife will never put her husband down or laugh at him but will greatly strengthen him and build him up, for God's glory. He will accomplish more by the power of her respect than he ever could on his own. That is why the word *respect* appears in verse 33. Respect breathes life into a man.

Here, then, is what we are seeing. Three times the New Testament reaffirms Genesis 2:24 as the permanent and praiseworthy definition of marriage. At the same time, the New Testament adds further insights and advances our understanding in striking ways. But there is nothing in the New Testament to suggest that the original vision of marriage in Genesis must, or even may, be set aside.

The New Testament brings the biblical love story to its final culmination in the Revelation of John. The apostle John does not quote Genesis 2:24, but his whole outlook is soaked through and through with Old Testament thought and imagery, including the marriage theme. Two of John's passages stand out. First:

> Then I heard what seemed to be the voice of a great multitude, like the roar of many waters and like the sound of mighty peals of thunder, crying out,
>
> > "Hallelujah!
> > For the Lord our God
> >   the Almighty reigns.
> > Let us rejoice and exult
> >   and give him the glory,
> > for the marriage of the Lamb has come,
> >   and his Bride has made herself ready;
> > it was granted her to clothe herself
> >   with fine linen, bright and pure"—
> > for the fine linen is the righteous deeds of the saints.
>
> And the angel said to me, "Write this: Blessed are those who are invited to the marriage supper of the Lamb." (Rev. 19:6–9a)

John contrasts "the great prostitute" (Rev. 17:1), which represents this corrupt and seductive world where anything goes, with the pure bride. For the world at the end of history, the party's over.

For the bride entering eternity, the wedding celebration has finally begun and will never end. In verses 1–4 of Revelation 19, John hears heaven exploding with praise for God's judgment upon the great prostitute. But God's servants on earth erupt in nuclear-powered praises for the final coming of the kingdom (v. 6) and the longed-for beginning of the marriage (v. 7).

The kingdom and the marriage are two aspects of the same reality, when God will finally be our all in all (1 Cor. 15:28), with no more distance, no more absence, no more waiting, but faith finally turned into sight, hope into possession, earthly sorrows into pleasures forevermore. The particular occasion for the church's powerful rejoicing here on her wedding day is that "his Bride has made herself ready" (v. 7). Unlike the marriage of the Lord with his old-covenant people Israel, which failed miserably, now the bride is so fully prepared for the approach of her glorious husband that she will be unable ever to spoil this eternal marriage. The church is at last "in splendor, without spot or wrinkle or any such thing," but she is "holy and without blemish" (Eph. 5:27).

How has the church finally become fit for her lover? The Revelation describes the path of authentic Christianity in bold ways. It speaks of patient endurance (Rev. 1:9), conquering the Accuser by the blood of the Lamb and by the word of our testimony and not loving our lives even unto death (Rev. 12:11), following the Lamb wherever he goes (Rev. 14:4), obeying God and keeping faith in Jesus (Rev. 14:12), and holding to the testimony of Jesus (Rev. 19:10). But here in Revelation 19:7–8, the bride has become presentable for the wedding celebration for two reasons.

For her part, according to verse 7, "his Bride has made herself ready." The gospel does not hesitate to say, "Let everyone who names the name of the Lord depart from iniquity" (2 Tim. 2:19).

The gospel calls us to cleanse ourselves from everything dishonorable (2 Tim. 2:21) and to reach by faith and repentance for everything excellent (2 Pet. 1:3–11). That is the bride's part, for the strong hope of that glorious wedding celebration above acts upon us now with purifying power (1 John 3:2–3). And it is important to see that the bride does not wait to prepare herself until after all her oppressors have been judged and dispensed with. It is later in this chapter that the King of kings and Lord of lords sweeps away "the kings of the earth," with "the beast" and "the false prophet" and all their remaining followers (Rev. 19:11–21). The church remains under pressure during her season of preparation. But her calling is not to defeat her enemies; her calling is to make herself ready for her groom.

For his part, our Savior graciously creates and sustains our readiness. He is at work in us, his power implied by the passive verb in verse 8: "It was granted her to clothe herself with . . . the righteous deeds of the saints." To escape the corruption of the great prostitute and to become prepared as the bride—this is "granted," God justifying us "by his grace as a gift" (Rom. 3:24) and "working in us that which is pleasing in his sight" (Heb. 13:21).[12] The final reason why the eternal romance will never be dimmed, but will only burn more brightly forever, is not in us but in our Lord. We engage with him, but he grants us even our sincerity of heart, and that is how we become prepared for the eternal wedding day.

Earlier in the Revelation, the great prostitute was "arrayed in purple and scarlet, and adorned with gold and jewels and pearls" (Rev. 17:4). The slut, tricked out in her worldly grandiosity, is dis-

---

12. G. K. Beale, *The Book of Revelation: A Commentary on the Greek Text* (Grand Rapids, MI: Eerdmans, 1999), 935, states it with more precise theological formulation: "Justification is the causal necessary condition for entrance into the eternal kingdom, but good works are a noncausal necessary condition." See Rom. 2:6–8.

gustingly drunk with the blood of the saints (Rev. 17:6). By contrast, the bride is dressed simply but gorgeously in "fine linen, bright and pure" (Rev. 19:8). Her wedding dress is neither showy nor drab, but beautiful with the only beauty that will never fade or fall out of fashion throughout the length of eternity. Whatever sins she committed in this life, she is now by God's grace "a pure virgin" (2 Cor. 11:2).

No surprise, then, that verse 9 concludes, "Blessed are those who are invited to the marriage supper of the Lamb." The word *blessed* is a congratulatory formula. It is what we cannot help saying when we see a highly desirable human ideal. The opposite of *blessed* is *woe*. That cry of doom and horror and revulsion is terrible: "Woe, woe, woe to those who dwell on the earth . . . !" (Rev. 8:13). Everyone without salvation in Christ will discover too late that all the joys of this fraudulent world only betray the hopes of the human heart. But true and lasting joy will endure and increase forever for all in Christ. There is no self-pity in the hearts of those invited into this marriage supper. There is no regret over earthly joys forsaken, "when the trials of the former days are forgotten in laughter and happiness around the table of the Lord."[13] This word *blessed* is saying, "Congratulations to everyone invited into this wedding celebration! How privileged and fortunate you are!" This word *blessed* helps us care a little bit less about the price we must pay to follow Jesus in this present evil age.[14] And notice that these hearty congratulations are announced to *all* believers. In verse 7, the church appears as "his Bride," a corporate singular. But in verses 8–9, John makes it personal to each and all of us with the plural "saints" and "those who are invited." The eternal

---

13. G. R. Beasley-Murray, *The Book of Revelation* (Grand Rapids, MI: Eerdmans, 1981), 274.
14. "Thus the NT beatitudes are not just intimations of the future or consolations in relation to it. They see the present in light of the future," according to Gerhard Kittel, ed., *Theological Dictionary of the New Testament* (Grand Rapids, MI: Eerdmans, 1967), 4:369.

promise is made to Christ's church as a whole and to all believers personally.

The other passage in John's Revelation sets our feet, so to speak, on the very brink of eternity, where we can see far into the future, as far as our vision is now able by faith to reach:

> Then I saw a new heaven and a new earth, for the first heaven and the first earth had passed away, and the sea was no more. And I saw the holy city, new Jerusalem, coming down out of heaven from God, prepared as a bride adorned for her husband. And I heard a loud voice from the throne saying, "Behold, the dwelling place of God is with man. He will dwell with them, and they will be his people, and God himself will be with them as their God. He will wipe away every tear from their eyes, and death shall be no more, neither shall there be mourning, nor crying, nor pain anymore, for the former things have passed away." And he who was seated on the throne said, "Behold, I am making all things new." (Rev. 21:1–5a)

One of the amazing things about the Bible is the grand scope of its vision. It begins with the creation of the heavens and the earth (Gen. 1:1), and it ends here with the re-creation of it all as a new heavens and a new earth. The Bible is nothing less than a history of the entire cosmos. And at each horizon of this grandeur is marriage: first the marriage of Adam and Eve, and now the wedding of the Lamb with his bride (Rev. 21:9).

Now the conflict is finally past, the victory is won, and peace descends. The sea disappears from view, for "the wicked are like the tossing sea; for it cannot be quiet, and its waters toss up mire and dirt" (Isa. 57:20). It was from this seething mass of restless mankind that the beast arose (Rev. 13:1). And the angel said to John, "The waters that you saw, where the prostitute is seated, are peoples and multitudes and nations and languages" (Rev. 17:15). But now the people of God need no longer brace themselves against the buffeting waves of this sea of human hostility, for the danger simply is not there anymore. A settled order of human shalom finally reigns.

But the perfect world we have always dreamed of will not rise from the earth as our achievement for our own glory. It will come down from God above for his glory alone: "And I saw the holy city, new Jerusalem, coming down out of heaven from God, prepared as a bride adorned for her husband" (Rev. 21:2). After every societal failure of mankind litters the course of human history—with brief flashes of brilliance here and there, but all of them eventually slipping into decline—the holy city, the sacred society, the new Jerusalem created by the miracle of God's grace will endure as the refuge of God's people. This city will not weary us with noise and stress; it will not defile us with corruption and pollution. This holy city will be an experience of romance, prepared as a bride, adorned in her wedding dress for her husband, suggesting intimacy and warmth and softness and joy and love and bliss as our constant experience there. Isaiah prophesied to Jerusalem, "As the bridegroom rejoices over the bride, so shall your God rejoice over you" (Isa. 62:5). Even so, it shall be—and forever.

Truly, the sufferings of this present time are not worth comparing with the glory that is to be revealed to us (Rom. 8:18). Our future is the only true measure of our present. Therefore, the prophecies of the Revelation might qualify as the most helpful parts of the Bible for struggling believers of today. That is the purpose of God's promises—to keep lifting our hearts with the buoyant power of a sure and certain hope. And what the ancient prophecies show us is that our future glory in Christ might be more human and familiar and delightful and, in a way, earthy than we had thought. But while we wait for the fulfillment of God's great plan, savoring by faith our future honeymoon with the Son of God, we are helped to stay true to him not by denying our sufferings but by comparing them with the glory that is to be revealed to us. One commentator puts it frankly: "Only in comparison with the new Jerusalem can the queenly splendors of Babylon be recognized as the seductive gauds of an old and raddled whore."[15] So much for this world! But it is Jonathan Edwards who draws back the veil to help us see more of the promised glory:

> In that resurrection morning, when the Sun of Righteousness shall appear in the heavens, shining in all his brightness and glory, he will come forth as a bridegroom; he shall come in the glory of his Father with all his holy angels. And at that glorious appearing of the great God and our Savior Jesus Christ shall the whole elect church, complete as to every individual member, and each member with the whole person, both body and soul, and both in perfect glory, ascend up to meet the Lord in the air, to be forever with the Lord. . . . Then will come the time when Christ will sweetly invite his spouse to enter in with him into the palace of his glory, which he had been preparing for her from the foundation of the world, and shall take her by the hand and lead her in with him; and this glorious bridegroom and bride shall, with all their shining ornaments, ascend up together into the heaven of heaven, the whole multitude of glorious angels waiting upon them; and this Son and daughter of God shall, in their united glory and joy, present themselves together before the Father;

15. G. B. Caird, *A Commentary on the Revelation of St. John the Divine* (London: Adam & Charles Black, 1966), 262.

. . . and they shall together receive the Father's blessing; and shall thenceforward rejoice together in consummate, uninterrupted, immutable and everlasting glory, in the love and embraces of each other, and in their shared enjoyment of the love of the Father.[16]

---

16. Jonathan Edwards, *Jonathan Edwards: Sermons and Discourses, 1743–1758*, ed. Wilson H. Kimnach (New Haven, CT: Yale University Press, 2006), 183–84. Style updated. I thank Dr. Dane Ortlund for drawing my attention to this section of Edwards.

4

Marriage in the World Today

If the Bible is telling us the truth about reality, then ultimacy is not cold, dark, blank space. Finality, in this universe we live in, is not cosmic emptiness going on and on forever, governed by no purpose, ruled by the laws of physics only, with no song, no poetry, no emotion, no laughter, no play, no love, no commitment, no sacrifice, no tears, and nothing humane and beautiful to live for and die for. If the Bible is telling us the truth about reality, then this horrible modern outlook is *completely* wrong, and the truth of our existence is the *opposite* of mechanistic nihilism.

If the Bible is telling us the truth about reality, then the universe we live in was created primarily with marital romance in mind. The heavens and the earth were created for the marriage of Adam and Eve. The new heavens and the new earth will be created for the marriage of Christ and his bride. The whole of cosmic reality exists as the venue for the eternal honeymoon of the perfect husband with his perfect bride in marital bliss forever and ever. This is the breathtaking claim of the Bible.

There is more at stake in marriage than we ever could have known, without the mystery revealed in the Christian gospel (Eph. 5:32). So as we conclude this study of marriage, let's think through some personal implications for our own lives. The implications are endless. But I will conclude with one momentous verse, relevant to all of us today: "Let marriage be held in honor among all, and let the marriage bed be undefiled, for God will judge the sexually immoral and adulterous" (Heb. 13:4). That was a countercultural message in the first century, and it is countercultural today. But it is one of the ways we offer to God acceptable worship with reverence and awe (Heb. 12:28).

The emphasis of the verse lies on the words "held in honor," that is, prized, valued, esteemed. The New Testament never says, "Let money be prized, valued, esteemed." But God has called us all to feel just that way about marriage. It is to be honored and lifted up and protected among all believers, not only among married believers. It is the God-defined institution of marriage as such, not only my own personal marriage, that I am to esteem. The gospel has shown us that every believer has something personally wonderful at stake in the sacred reality of marriage, as it points beyond itself to the endless love of Jesus for us all. Now God wants all of us to translate that new awareness into the active hallowing of marriage here in this world.

The gospel, when it is allowed to make its own natural impact, creates a pro-marriage culture among God's people. Not that unmarried people are second-class, for single people living for Christ gain strategic advantages over married people (1 Cor. 7:25-35). But marriage bespeaks ultimate reality in a way that the single life does not. It was designed to. Human marriage has always been intended by God to serve as a prophetic whisper of the eternal marriage. Every real marriage in the world today makes that statement, to some degree, however weakly, because that is what marriage *is*. Very few realities in our lives bear such a sacred meaning and deserve such special consideration.

All churches, therefore, have a gospel-motivated obligation actively to teach and honor and promote marriage, for the display of the gospel in our world of confusion and despair. If we love the preaching of the gospel from pulpits, then we will also love the display of the gospel in marriages. Churches must not be neutral or casual about what so rejoices the heart of God.

Yes, marriage also provides social benefits, which both believers and unbelievers can appreciate, especially the rearing of children for the next generation in a secure and stable environment. For that reason alone, the state has a clear interest in supporting and protecting the institution of marriage. Marriage is not the private property of the Christian church. At the creation, God gave marriage to the entire human race. But no one, and not even the entire human race all together, has the right to redefine marriage on its own terms. Nor can anyone, or all of us together, however broad and even unanimous our consensus, expect marriage to succeed if it is reshaped according to what it never was and can never be. If the state fails in its duty to preserve and protect real marriage, there will be a personal, social, and historic cost, a painful and heavy human cost.

The United States Supreme Court, in the landmark case Obergefell versus Hodges on June 26, 2015, by a vote of five to four, ruled that the US Constitution guarantees a right to same-sex "marriage." Writing in the *New York Times*, Adam Liptak explained that in this and other related cases "Justice Kennedy embraced a vision of a living Constitution, one that evolves with societal changes."[1] (The reporter's candor reminds us that college English and literature and

---

1. "Supreme Court Ruling Makes Same-Sex Marriage a Right Nationwide," http://www.ny times.com/2015/06/27/us/supreme-court-same-sex-marriage.html.

hermeneutics courses might be shaping the future of our world as powerfully as political science courses do.) But as damaging as that Supreme Court ruling is, and as ominous for the future, the state has been injuring a pro-marriage culture for decades. In 1969 Governor Ronald Reagan of California made what he later admitted was one of the biggest mistakes of his political life when he signed into effect the nation's first no-fault divorce law, with other states following soon thereafter. The state made it easier to end a marriage in divorce, and so it was.[2] But even as the state foolishly continues to undermine a pro-marriage culture, our churches must work all the harder to build a pro-marriage counterculture, where faithfulness and beauty and lasting love point the way not only to a better human society but also, and far more, to the eternal love of Christ.

Divorce grieves the heart of God. By now, having surveyed the biblical love story, we know why God feels so strongly in favor of solidly happy marriages. We know how precious marriage is to the Father and how Christ longs for his own with all the romantic passion of his mighty heart. If that gospel is the true drama of human history, and it is, then how could God *not* hate divorce and every injury we inflict on his precious gift of marriage? God does not hate divorced people. He does not hate gay people. He does not hate Supreme Court justices. He does not hate you and me. Fortunately for us all, "for God so loved the world, that he gave his only Son, that whoever believes in him should not perish but have eternal life" (John 3:16). But God's people who have been divorced and gay and mistaken in many ways, that is, all believers in Christ—it is spiritual whores like us, having fallen exhausted and guilty into the arms of

---

2. W. Bradford Wilcox, "The Evolution of Divorce," *National Affairs* 1 (Fall 2009): 81–94. Wilcox tracks the shift in our culture over recent decades from "the institutional model of marriage," with its stable, dutiful, child-rearing values, to "the soul-mate model of marriage," with its emphasis on personal fulfillment, emotional intensity, and even duty to self. Neither of these models of marriage measures up to the profound mystery of gospel marriage.

our Bridegroom, who can now be compelling voices in favor of marriage. We know by experience the sorrows of every departure from God's beautiful norm. Indeed, if Jonathan Edwards is right, if brokenhearted people make the best Christians,[3] then we who have not lived up to God's high standards for marriage and sexuality can serve best as advocates for those very standards. May our voices be humble but clear.

Hebrews 13:4 also says that the marriage bed must be undefiled, kept pure, its joys richly cultivated and its parameters strictly guarded. Why? We have seen that the biblical concern about sexual integrity is not a petty Victorian taboo, as if sex were dirty or even just beneath true spirituality. Just the opposite. Married sex, with its intimacy and desire and pleasure and intensity and adoration and satisfaction and rest, is a glorious metaphor of heaven. To betray our Lord's sexual ethics, to drag his amazing gift into the gutter, is to deny the most sacred reality of all, the marriage of the Lamb, given his prophetic purpose invested in married sexuality. For God *not* to judge sexual sin would be for God to trivialize his own blood-bought purposes.

Everyone who reveres the gospel has compelling reasons to champion biblical sexual ethics. It is falling to our generation to raise up a prophetic counterculture in the face of the sexual revolution's direct attack on Christ and his marital appeal at the heart of the gospel. The fact that we too are sinners does not exempt us from taking this stand. Our own sinfulness simply means that we take our stand with humility and honesty. But we must not be silent. What is at stake in our sexuality is nothing less than the gospel itself.

We need a massive spiritual cleansing coming down from above

---

3. See the quote from Edwards on pages 54–55.

upon our generation, because a tsunami of sexual defilement has slammed us in the face. For example, every Christian man and woman who cannot stop looking at Internet pornography must have the humility to go to his or her pastor and say, "Pastor, I have a problem. I'm out of control. I am viewing, and thereby participating in, the violation of women and children. I am living in active denial of my Savior and everything he stands for. I love the Lord. But I can't stop. I don't make sense to myself. I need help." As the Holy Spirit renews our vision of our own sexuality, married and single, men and women, and as the Spirit stirs our hearts to care more about the glory of the Lord than our own face saving, the pastors of our churches today will be wonderfully swamped with inquiries from honest sinners longing to be clean again.

The blood of Jesus, God's Son, powerfully cleanses from all sin (1 John 1:7). But nothing will change until we get radical. Why not stop posing? Why not stop today? Why not face our sexual sins without a moment's further delay and fight together by faith for the recovery of our integrity before the Lord?[4] Again, it is *sinners* whom God wants to use in this generation. Sin as such does not disqualify us; it is only unconfessed sin that disqualifies us. But the blood of Jesus wonderfully cleanses away every sin that we will honestly confront within the community of a safe, gospel-centered church. When the world sees more repentance in our churches, our churches will see more repentance in the world.

If the Bible is telling us the truth about reality, then Ryan Anderson is not overstating the matter when he calls every one of us to rebuild in the present for the sake of the future, whatever the cost to us today:

---

4. See John Piper, "Gutsy Guilt," http://www.christianitytoday.com/ct/2007/october/38.72.html.

The church needs to find a way to capture the moral imagination of the next generation. It needs to make the truth about human sexuality and its fulfillment in marriage not only attractive and appealing, but noble and exhilarating. This is a truth worth staking one's life on.[5]

If the Bible is telling us the truth about reality, then the time has come for all Christians and churches to pray for power, to think with clarity, to confess with humility, and to shout with joy on behalf of God's priceless, blood-bought gift of marriage.

And to God alone be all the glory forever.

---

5. Ryan T. Anderson, http://www.canonandculture.com/rebuilding-a-marriage-culture-a-fourfold-mission-for-the-church/.

For Further Reading

Allberry, Sam. *Is God Anti-Gay?* Croydon, UK: Good Book Company, 2013.

Andreades, Sam A. *enGendered: God's Gift of Gender Difference in Relationship.* Wooster, OH: Weaver, 2015.

Girgis, Sherif, Ryan T. Anderson, and Robert P. George. *What Is Marriage? Man and Woman: A Defense.* New York: Encounter, 2012.

Haleem, M. A. S. Abdel. *The Qur'an.* Oxford, UK: Oxford University Press, 2010.

Heidel, Alexander. *The Babylonian Genesis: The Story of the Creation.* Chicago: University of Chicago Press, 1951.

Ortlund, Raymond C., Jr. *God's Unfaithful Wife: A Biblical Theology of Spiritual Adultery*, New Studies in Biblical Theology 2. Downers Grove, IL: InterVarsity Press, 1996.

Piper, John, and Wayne Grudem, eds. *Recovering Biblical Manhood and Womanhood.* Wheaton, IL: Crossway, 1991.

Stienstra, Nelly. *YHWH Is the Husband of His People: Analysis of a Biblical Metaphor with Special Reference to Translation.* Kampen, NL: Kok Pharos, 1993.

Waltke, Bruce K. *An Old Testament Theology: An Exegetical, Canonical and Thematic Approach.* Grand Rapids, MI: Zondervan, 2007.

General Index

Scripture Index

Short Studies in Biblical Theology Series

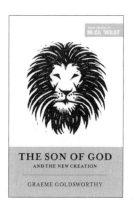

THE SON OF GOD
AND THE NEW CREATION

GRAEME GOLDSWORTHY

MARRIAGE
AND THE MYSTERY OF THE GOSPEL

RAY ORTLUND

WORK
AND OUR LABOR IN THE LORD

JAMES M. HAMILTON JR.

COVENANT
AND GOD'S PURPOSE FOR THE WORLD

THOMAS R. SCHREINER

THE KINGDOM OF GOD
AND THE GLORY OF THE CROSS

PATRICK SCHREINER

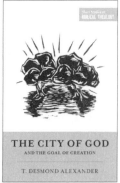

THE CITY OF GOD
AND THE GOAL OF CREATION

T. DESMOND ALEXANDER

For more information, visit crossway.org/ssbt.